The Word at War

The Word at War

World War Two in 100 Phrases

Philip Gooden and Peter Lewis

Bloomsbury Information
An imprint of Bloomsbury Publishing Plc

B L O O M S B U R Y
LONDON · NEW DELHI · NEW YORK · SYDNEY

Bloomsbury Information

An imprint of Bloomsbury Publishing Plc

1385 Broadway	50 Bedford Square
New York	London
NY 10018	WC1B 3DP
USA	UK

www.bloomsbury.com

**BLOOMSBURY and the Diana logo are trademarks of
Bloomsbury Publishing Plc**

First published 2014
First published in paperback 2015

Library of Congress Cataloging-in-Publication Data
A catalog record for this book is available from the Library of Congress.

ISBN: HB:	978-1-4729-0489-8
PB:	978-1-4729-2248-9
ePUB:	978-1-4729-0490-4
ePDF:	978-1-4729-0491-1

Design by Fiona Pike, Pike Design, Winchester
Typeset by Hewer Text UK Ltd, Edinburgh
Printed and bound in Great Britain

The authors, Peter Lewis and Philip Gooden, dedicate this book to John Desmond Lewis (b.1922) and Douglas Wyndham-Harris (b.1918), father and father-in-law respectively. They lived and fought through all this.

War is commonly held to be the mother of invention
where military technology is concerned. Our book, we hope,
will show this to be equally true of words and phrases.

Contents

Introduction

World War Two continues to be a hugely popular topic in all forms of media. American film and television blockbusters like *Saving Private Ryan* and *Band of Brothers* commemorate acts of heroism during the conflict that writer Studs Terkel dubbed 'The Good War'. British culture is steeped in nostalgia for our plucky stand against Nazi tyranny: witness the evergreen appeal of the sitcom *Dad's Army* and the recent recycling of the 1939 Ministry of Information poster 'Keep Calm and Carry On' into everything from mugs and baby clothes to flight bags and iPad cases. In Germany and Austria, too, it is a hot topic, though understandably treated very differently – one need only think of the Oscar-winning 2004 film *Downfall* (*Der Untergang*).

More than this, though, the terminology of the war has embedded itself in our collective psyche; British politicians are fond of invoking the 'Dunkirk spirit' whenever the country is faced with major crisis or even minor adversity, and Roosevelt's famous description of Pearl Harbor as 'a date which will live in infamy' was echoed by many US commentators after the 9/11 attacks. War words also resonate throughout popular culture: in the 2000s, the Shepherd Neame brewery ran an inventive and amusing advertising campaign for its Spitfire Ale ('The Bottle of Britain'), featuring posters with slogans such as 'Not for Messrs Schmidt' and 'Downed all over Kent, just like the Luftwaffe'. In the same vein, we berate tiresome jobsworths as 'little Hitlers', while English football fans taunt their German opposite numbers with the tasteless chant: 'There's only one Bomber Harris!'

So, all extremely well-trodden territory. Or is it? How many of us realise, for instance, that the poster 'Keep Calm and Carry On', far from achieving its morale-boosting aim, never actually appeared on Britain's streets? Or know what a 'sib' was in wartime propaganda? Or have any idea why, well into the 1980s, Bavaria was still distributing to its schools a contemporary atlas showing the long-defunct 'Greater Germany', with the country's borders as at 1937? This is where *The Word at War* comes in. We have cherry-picked words and phrases spawned and popularised in the lead-up to World War Two and during the conflict itself.

The Word at War comprises 15 chapters, organised in roughly chronological order, and discussing different aspects of the conflict. Within each of these, essays explore and explain the derivations of, and the stories behind, popular terms and phraseology of the period. The scope of the book goes beyond Britain and the United States to investigate the use and abuse of language in other combatant nations; the terminology of totalitarian regimes like Nazi Germany, Fascist Italy or Pétain's Vichy France gives a fascinating insight into the social and political order prevailing there.

Chapter 1

The Legacy of World War One

An examination of some of the linguistic terms which were created at the very beginning of the 20th century shows that there were premonitions of the catastrophes to come, verbal tremors of two mighty global conflicts. Whether in areas such as weaponry and the armed forces or espionage and counter-intelligence, or the expansion of warfare to include the civilian population, we find newly created words or new formulations of old ones, each pointing the way towards the new century. It is a century which will outrank the destructive record of any previous period in terms of the sheer numbers of casualties and a worldwide engagement, one from which almost no country will emerge unscathed. And the profound consequences have endured to the present day . . .

Civilian Collateral

[British: Concentration camps]

For early examples of linguistic innovation in 20th-century warfare, take the decisive impact that Herbert Horatio Kitchener had on the prosecution of the Boer War (1899–1902). This conflict produced initial defeats for Britain at the hands of two independent statelets occupied by the descendants of the original Dutch settlers of southern Africa. When Britain eventually annexed the Boers' territory, widespread guerrilla activity continued only for it to be ruthlessly suppressed by Lord Kitchener, a Commander-in-Chief who was well-versed in other colonial campaigns on the continent.

One of Kitchener's contributions was the creation of the blockhouse system, used to partition the country and so make it easier to control enemy movement. More pernicious was Kitchener's other innovation: the concentration camp (the term first noted in English in 1901). Civilian populations, both Boer and Black African, were forced into these tented camps. The Boer internees were principally women and children expelled from their homes and farms, which were then subjected to a 'scorched earth' policy so as to deprive the male fighters of provisions and shelter. Conditions were very poor, and disease and malnutrition were rife with about a third of the inhabitants dying as a result. That there was an intentionally punitive element in the concentration camp system is shown by the fact that the families of men who were still fighting received even less food than the other occupants.

The link with the Nazi camps or *Konzentrationslager* is more than nominal, and lies not merely in the indifference or brutality with which the inmates were treated but in the targeting of a specific ethnic group in clearing whole regions. The term 'ethnic cleansing' was not coined until the close of the 20th century but the actions of the British military against the Boer population in southern Africa can accurately be labelled as such. (It is interesting that the term 'bittereinders', used to describe the Boer fighters who held out against the British until the end, resurfaced after the 2003 invasion of Iraq, when those who continued to resist the US occupation and settlement were referred to as 'bitter enders' or 'dead-enders'.)

The mistreatment of civilians, extending to their deliberate slaughter, is as old as warfare, but the phrase 'civilian casualty' first appears with an almost uncanny aptness at the exact start of the 20th century. Although there was widespread unease and some protest about the British treatment of non-combatant Boers, the term is used not about the war in southern Africa but appears in an American newspaper in connection with the Boxer rebellion in China, the uprising against the presence of imperial powers (Britain, Germany, Russia) on Chinese territory. This first use of 'civilian casualty' ushered in a period which saw war-related deaths occur on an unprecedented scale among the non-combatant populations of warring nations. Estimates are notoriously sketchy but amount to nearly eight million dead for World War One and, when the concentration camp deaths are included, twenty-eight million for World War Two.

Things to Come
[British: Missile/Atom bomb]

There are two unrelated ways in which the slaughter of civilians could be said to be new in the 20th century, not because humanity had become more murderous but because the means to bring about deaths on such a large scale were not available before 1900. The first was the application of industrial-scale methods and bureaucratic systems to genocidal ends. The second lay in the capacity to launch attacks from the air. From the early 20th century, the civilians of one country could be directly reached by their enemies in another, even though these non-combatants might be hundreds – and eventually thousands – of miles from any front line. Of course, civilian populations have always been affected by, and often suffered from, wars which are being fought at a distance from them, but the rapid advances in flight and the possibilities which technology opened up for aerial warfare brought the fighting home, literally. The death and dilapidation which followed was not gradual like, say, the effect produced by the Allies' naval blockade of Germany in World War One, but was immediate and terrifying.

Civilian fear of air attack was a prominent feature of both world wars and, in the run-up to the outbreak of hostilities in 1939, it led to an almost paralysing sense of doom among some British politicians and planners. 'The bomber will always get through,' was the fatalistic approach of Stanley Baldwin, three times Prime Minister in the interwar period, while as apprehension rose to a peak in the late 30s, a highly respected military theorist expected that there would be 250,000 casualties in the first week of war alone.

It was the writer H.G. Wells in his futurist novel *The War in the Air* (1908) who seems to have come up with the phrase 'air power', a formulation along the lines of 'sea power', itself an early Victorian coinage to describe Britain's supremacy of the oceans. Wells, by contrast, applies the 'air power' expression to Germany. In the same book he refers to 'flying-machine raids'. He had always been conscious of the threat from above and the destruction which could rain down, almost without warning, on people going about their daily lives.*

Wells was one of the earliest writers to employ 'missile' in its modern sense, in his famous science-fiction novel *The War of the Worlds* (1897): 'One night (the first missile [from Mars] then could scarcely have been 10,000,000 miles away) I went for a walk with my wife.' This ever-prescient writer was certainly the first to use 'atomic' (in 1914) to describe both a means of propulsion and the principle behind a new type of bomb. It was also Wells who turned the German name of the inventor of the dirigible airship into a verb meaning 'to drop bombs from a Zeppelin'. And it was from just such an airship, the creation of Count Ferdinand von Zeppelin, that the first aerial bombs in history were dropped on 6 August 1914, two days after the British declaration of war on Germany. The inhabitants of Liège in Belgium were on the receiving end of the cargo a Zeppelin despatched from Cologne. Thirteen bombs were released; nine civilians died.

The 20th century had begun.

*Popular fear of aerial bombardment prior to World War Two was stoked by the dystopian feature film *Things to Come* (1936; directed by Alexander Korda), for which Wells wrote the screenplay. It begins with a bombing raid on the British city of 'Everytown', on Christmas night, 1940, in which poison gas is used.

Forces' Favourite

[German/British: 'Lili Marleen'/'Lili Marlene']

Famed as a favourite song of both German and Allied troops in World War Two, 'Lili Marleen' began life as a poem by the German writer Hans Leip (1893–1983). Leip served from 1915–17 on the Eastern Front and in the Carpathians, and it was during his first year of combat that he wrote the verse for his girlfriend. It was variously entitled *Lied eines jungen Wachpostens* or *Das Lied eines jungen Soldaten auf der Wacht* (both meaning 'Song of a Young Sentry'). The sentiment of the poem is wistful and melancholic, as the soldier anticipates falling in battle and never returning to his loved one.

Leip's poem was first set to music by the film-music composer Norbert Schultze in 1938 and recorded by German singer Lale Andersen on 2 August 1939. Sales were initially disappointing (around only 700 in two years), and it was in fact a chance event that propelled the song to worldwide fame. In 1941, a Wehrmacht lieutenant charged with compiling a playlist for the German forces' radio station in occupied Yugoslavia (*Soldatensender Belgrad*) came across Andersen's recording and made it the tune with which the station signed off every night at 21.55–22.00 hours. *Soldatensender Belgrad* was heard throughout the Mediterranean, and the song gained a huge following, especially among troops of the Afrika Korps, who requested it ever more frequently. Joseph Goebbels hated the distinctly unmartial, implicitly anti-war tone of 'Lili Marleen'* and, as Propaganda Minister in charge of all broadcasting, banned Andersen from performing it. Afrika Korps commander Erwin Rommel, on the other hand, liked it and backed his men's request, and the song's popularity kept growing to the point where Goebbels was forced to relent.

Nor was its meteoric rise to fame confined to Germany; men of the Eighth Army and US forces in the Western Desert tuned in to the Belgrade station especially to hear it, and even learnt its German words. Some British commanders, no doubt mindful of the old adage that the devil has all the best tunes, were concerned that it might undermine morale, but the oddness of squaddies going round singing in German was solved when Tommie Connor provided English lyrics for it in 1944 (American songwriter Mack David had written his own set the year before). Connor's version was immediately recorded by Anne Shelton, and then by 'Forces' Sweetheart' Vera Lynn, while that same year saw a US version released by the double-act of Bing Crosby and Doris Day. Meanwhile, Marlene Dietrich, resident in America throughout the war, gave her own distinctively flat rendition of the song in both languages.

*In Rainer Werner Fassbinder's 1980 film *Lili Marleen*, the figure of Goebbels goes so far as to call the tune *Das Lied mit dem Totentanzgeruch* ('that song redolent of the Dance of Death'). This may, of course, be less documentary fact than poetic licence on the director's part.

Hitler's Whopper

[German: *der Dolchstoß*, 'Stab in the back'/ *die Große Lüge*, 'the Big Lie']

A key shot in the rhetorical locker of demagogues is the Big Lie*: repeat it often and loudly enough, so the theory goes, and the masses will eventually swallow it. Two outrageous whoppers from the 20th century are Mao Zedong's 'Great Leap Forward' (a programme of economic reform which failed dismally) and Margaret Thatcher's 'There Is No Alternative' (there most certainly was). One of Adolf Hitler's favourites, in a political career built on self-delusion and mendacity, was the myth of the *Dolchstoß* (literally: 'dagger thrust'; usually rendered as 'stab in the back'). This was the claim that Germany had been defeated in World War One not by force of arms but by an act of treachery on the part of craven socialist and liberal politicians. Nazi demonology predictably identified these dark forces as Jewish.

The figure most closely associated with the *Dolchstoßlegende* is Erich von Ludendorff, the wartime German Chief of Staff and later Nazi fellow-traveller (see Chapter 13: A Defiant Detour). In the autumn of 1919, while dining with the head of the British Military Mission in Berlin, Major-General Sir Neill Malcolm, Ludendorff responded to his host's enquiry as to why Germany lost the war with a litany of complaints about politicians. He then eagerly seized on Malcolm's question 'You mean that you were stabbed in the back?' by responding 'Yes, that's it exactly – we were stabbed in the back!' Before long, the phrase had become a mantra among far-right factions in the Weimar Republic, a standing grievance against the Leftist traitors (the so-called *Novemberverbrecher*, or 'November criminals') who had allegedly sold their country and its fighting men short. The unvarnished truth was that, after Ludendorff's Spring Offensive of 1918 had run into the sand, the Imperial German Army was a busted flush.

Far worse than merely skewing historical fact, though, by suggesting that a conspiracy of Jews had forced Germany's humiliating surrender, the myth traduced the great sacrifice made by the 100,000 or more Jewish servicemen who had fought for their country alongside their Gentile compatriots. Twelve thousand of them paid with their lives; visit any German military cemetery on the Western Front, and the many graves marked with the Star of David give the lie to that vile Big Lie.

Fascist Italy had its own version of the *Dolchstoßlegende*. Of course, this was not created to explain away defeat, since the country had fought with the Allies in World War One. In 1915, a secret pact (the Treaty of London) was made by France, Britain and Russia to persuade Italy to weigh in on their side, promising it major territorial gains, especially along the

Dalmatian coast, in the event of an Allied victory. This agreement was summarily reneged upon in the 1919 Treaty of Versailles, with Italy obtaining far less of the former Austro-Hungarian empire than it had expected. Irredentists and Mussolini's Fascists railed bitterly against this broken pledge as the *vittoria mutilata*, the 'mutilated victory'. Inevitably, the phrase itself can be traced back to Gabriele d'Annunzio (*see* Chapter 3: Lauding the *Duce*; Chapter 10: A Political Purgative).

*It was Hitler who coined this very phrase ('*Große Lüge*') in 1925. In *Mein Kampf* (Vol 1, Ch. X) he accused the Jews of employing just such a technique, and explained its rationale in the following terms: '. . . *the broad masses of a nation are always more easily corrupted in the deeper strata of their emotional nature than consciously or voluntarily; and thus in the primitive simplicity of their minds they more readily fall victims to the big lie than the small lie* . . .' Ironically, Hitler's specific charge was that it had been used to unfairly lay the blame for German defeat in 1918 at Ludendorff's door. A wonderful instance of a Big Lie being spread even as the term was being defined.

Chapter 2

Appeasement and the Phoney War

A few days before the outbreak of war, the poet W.H. Auden, sitting in a bar on Fifty-Second Street, mused on the decade which was just ending and voiced his fears at the darkening future. In the poem 'September 1, 1939', he dismissed the 1930s as 'a low dishonest decade' while even in the comparative safety and liberty of New York, he felt how an 'odour of death/Offends the September night'. This bleak moment had been a long time coming; Mussolini became the Italian Prime Minister as early as 1922 while Hitler was elected Chancellor of Germany in 1933. To quote the title of another poem by Auden, the 1930s were a true 'Age of Anxiety'.

Friends of the Führer
[British: Mosleyites; Blackshirts]

From the moment Hitler gained power in Germany, there was no shortage in Britain of admirers, acolytes and apologists for him and for Nazi rule in general. The motives of the sympathisers were mixed. Some felt uncomfortable about the punitive way Germany had been treated after the 1919 Versailles settlement and welcomed the new mood of unity, patriotism and purpose which Hitler alone seemed capable of instilling in his people. This tolerance was even extended to alarming signs of national self-assertion such as the reoccupation of the Rhineland (1936). Others went into contortions to accommodate and justify Hitler because they feared the prospect of another war and so gave the Führer the benefit of the doubt until his ambition and ruthlessness could no longer be denied.

For many, Bolshevism was a far greater threat than Fascism and a revitalised Germany had the potential to be 'the bulwark against Communism in Europe', as David Lloyd George put it in parliament in 1934. Others were impatient or cynical with the failures of the democratic system, particularly in the economic and social crisis following the 1929 Wall Street Crash, and they applauded the appearance of a European strongman who could sidestep – or, more likely, kick aside – the ballot box. Hitler might cut democratic corners but he built roads and houses, didn't he? Above all, he restored order to society. Mussolini had been fawned over in similar terms.

In the welcome for Hitler and approval of Nazi behaviour there was a strong streak of anti-Semitism. Indeed, this could be linked to hostility to Communism, which was often seen as an ideology with strong Jewish connections from its Marxist beginnings to its Trotskyite deviations. Nevertheless, anti-Semitism had always been a 'minority interest in Great Britain', according to Richard Griffiths in *Fellow Travellers of the Right* (1980), despite the existence of 'widespread parlour anti-Semitism, and verbal anti-Semitism'. But Hitler's ascendancy gave licence to some to say and write what they might otherwise have kept hidden. As early as 1933, Hitler was complimented for limiting the Jewish influence which, according to *The Patriot* magazine, 'had become excessive and injurious'. In an explanation which is still dismally familiar in the world of conspiracists, the same magazine noted that anti-German propaganda was the result of a 'wonderful organisation of Jewish power in all lands for the protection of racial interests'. More widely, there was a feeling that the nations of northern Europe such as Britain and Germany shared a common ancestry (*see* Chapter 3: White Power) which not only distinguished them from, but made them superior to, more suspect and exotic cultures.

There was yet another strand in British attitudes towards Hitler which amounted to hero-worship. At best this emerges as naivety, as when an MP commented after meeting Herr Hitler: '. . . peace and justice are the key words of his policy.' At worst, it is knee-trembling infatuation. The poster girl here is Unity Mitford, one of the daughters of Lord Redesdale, for whom Hitler was 'a right-thinking man of irreproachable sincerity and honesty'. Unity went a few steps further. She became one of the Führer's circle and carried her enthusiasm back to England, saluting the postmistress in her home village of Swinbrook, Oxfordshire with a raised arm and a cry of 'Heil Hitler!'

Diana Mitford, one of Unity's sisters, married Oswald Mosley, the founder of the British Union of Fascists (BUF), which in its early days seemed more aligned with Mussolini's brand of fascism. In 1936, the BUF became the British Union of Fascists and National Socialists and the movement's flag, previously adorned with the Italianate fasces, now featured a single lightning-bolt, reminiscent of SS insignia.

Mosley was the best-known pro-Nazi in Britain and, from the early 1930s, his supporters were sometimes referred to as Mosleyites. Borrowing the black, militaristic garb worn by

Mussolini's thuggish followers, they were also known as Blackshirts (originally after the Italian *camicie nere*) while the organisation's magazine was titled *The Blackshirt*. The word took some some time to acquire its overtones of sinister absurdity and once had a certain dash* to it, in keeping with Mosley's flamboyant, if flaky, reputation. Initially he and his movement attracted supporters on both left and right, with Lord Rothermere's *Daily Mail* headlining an article of January 1934 'Hurrah for the Blackshirts' and claiming that the 'well-organised' BUF was 'ready to take over responsibility for national affairs with the same directness of purpose and energy of method as Hitler and Mussolini have displayed'. After that it was downhill all the way, with Mosley's less rabid backers falling off and glimpses of the real BUF in its reflexive anti-Semitism and taste for street violence. Soon after the outbreak of war, Mosley and his wife were interned under Defence Regulation 18b, usually known simply as 18b, which provided for the detention of fascist sympathisers without trial.

*Beginning in 1925 Graham M. Jeffries, a now forgotten British thriller writer, produced a series of books which featured Blackshirt, a 'gentleman crook'.

An Array of Oddballs

[British: Imperial Fascist League/The Link/ The English Mistery/The English Array]

There were several other groups which combined dissatisfaction with the existing state of affairs in Britain, admiration for at least some aspects of Nazi Germany, and standard anti-Semitism. The Imperial Fascist League, founded by a veterinary surgeon who specialised in camel diseases, had the distinction of adopting the swastika (with a Union Jack background) as its emblem. Slightly less compromised was the Link, an organisation devoted to Anglo-German friendship and one which grew in strength as a war became more likely. This was a decentralised operation and some of the provincial branches of the Link indulged in nothing more than German beer and food evenings but others were treated to talks with titles like 'Secret Forces Working for War', the usual nudging reference to behind-the-scenes manipulation of world affairs by Jews and Freemasons (a fantasy alliance sometimes shortened to 'Jud-Mas').

On the fringes were groups whose titles alone suggested that their founders and members found 20th-century life a profoundly disturbing experience. The name of the Paladin League, founded by Lt-Col. Graham Seton Hutchison in 1930, is indicative of a hankering for a golden, medieval past. (A paladin was a chivalrous knight, straight out of legend.) A couple of years afterwards, Hutchison flew to the other end of the spectrum and formed the National Workers' Movement, later the National Socialist Workers' Party. He was probably involved too in the English Mistery (sic). This was a back-to-feudal-basics outfit, intended to set standards 'for districts, villages and crafts and trades'. One of its leaders, Lord Lymington, declared: 'We did not regard ourselves as *Herrenvolk* ['the master race'] but we wanted our revival to be Anglo-Saxon in the sense that Alfred the Great was Anglo-Saxon.' Fringe parties of the right are as ready to split as those on the far left, and within a few years Lymington had fallen out with the founder of the Mistery and set up the English Array. Membership of the Array was concentrated among landowners, often titled ones, but interest in questions of soil and nutrition did not preclude justification in their *Quarterly Gazette* of Hitler's occupation of Czechoslovakia (1938) as well as anti-Semitic slurs. The regressive nature of the Array is shown by their camp, grandiloquent ranks: Lymington himself was Marshal of the Array, and other titles included Steward of the Fens and Lieutenant of the King Alfred Muster in Dorset.

Nazis Across the Pond
[American: The Bund]

In the United States was a substantial group which, while not pro-Hitler, nevertheless believed that the country had no business fighting wars in Europe. After all, it was scarcely 20 years since they had been dragged into involvement in the last one. At its peak, the America First movement numbered some 80,000 members, including the President's cousin, Theodore Roosevelt Jr., while the influential segment of the press under the control of William Randolph Hearst also took up an isolationist stance.

But there were some unabashed and high-profile supporters of Hitler, including Charles A. Lindbergh,* the first man to fly solo across the Atlantic, and the industrialist Henry Ford, creator of the Model T. In 1938, both men were awarded the Service Cross of the German Eagle, a swastika-embellished gold medallion presented to foreigners for services to the Reich. Approval at home was far from universal; the US Secretary of the Interior referred to the medallions as 'tokens of contemptuous distinction', and despite the resonant names of Ford and Lindbergh, the pro-fascist movements in America achieved even less than they managed in Britain.

The best known and most active of the American groups was the German-American Bund (*Amerikadeutscher Volksbund*) or, simply, the Bund (i.e. confederation). This was established by Fritz Kuhn, a Munich-born veteran of World War One who emigrated to the US in 1927 and who was elected *Bundesführer* in 1936. But the Bund's swastika paraphernalia, tireless Sieg-heiling and anti-Semitic propaganda turned out to be so counterproductive, stirring up anti-German feeling among Americans, that the German government prohibited its own citizens from becoming members and banned the organisation from using Nazi emblems and symbols. The highpoint of the Bund was a 1939 rally in Madison Square Garden that attracted more than 20,000 people and featured a series of speeches whose tolerantly inclusive style can be judged from the introductory words of G. Wilhelm Kunze, the Bund's National Public Relations Director:

> *Mein Bundesführer, OD-Men** who help us SECURE our right to peaceable assembly and free speech, Bund-Members, our Boys and Girls, Fellow White Americans and other Non-Parasitic Guests . . .*

In the same year as the Madison Square rally Kuhn was convicted of tax evasion and fraud and, with the advent of war in Europe, the Bund withered away.

*In Philip Roth's counterfactual novel *The Plot Against America* (2005), Charles Lindbergh turns from national hero into presidential candidate. On an isolationist ticket, he defeats Franklin D. Roosevelt by a landslide in the 1940 election. His term in the White House is marked not only by a rapprochement with Nazi Germany – Lindbergh and Hitler sign a non-aggression pact at a summit in Iceland in 1941 – but by an

insidious campaign of anti-Semitism in which Jews are to lose their distinctiveness under the Office of American Absorption. The plot twist near the end, whereby Roth restores American – and global – history to its proper course, is both unexpected and plausible.
**OD-Men: the *Ordnungsdienst* ('Order Division') were the Bund's storm troopers, like Hitler's SA or Mosley's Blackshirts, and were responsible for order at meetings or, properly speaking, the intimidation of their opponents.

Pieces of Paper

[British: Munich Agreement]

Munich had a special resonance for the Allies, particularly the British. It was there that a four-power conference was held at the end of September 1938 to decide the fate of Czechoslovakia. Hitler, Mussolini and the Prime Ministers of Britain (Chamberlain) and France (Daladier) met to decide the terms on which the western German-speaking part of Czechoslovakia, the Sudetenland, would be handed over to Nazi Germany. The agreement, in which the Czechs had no say, averted war for the time being while a further piece of paper, relating only to Anglo-German relations, enabled Neville Chamberlain to return in triumph to London claiming 'peace for our time'. At Heston Aerodrome, he stepped out of the cabin of the British Airways airliner that had brought him from Germany and famously announced: 'This morning I had another talk with the German Chancellor, Herr Hitler, and here is the paper which bears his name upon it as well as mine.' Unfortunately, it soon became clear that the agreement wasn't worth the paper it was written on. Widespread relief was followed by scepticism and the realisation that Czechoslovakia would not be the end of Hitler's territorial ambitions.

The very word 'Munich' rapidly became shorthand for appeasement and betrayal. A story told by Leonard Mosley in his history of the period, *On Borrowed Time* (1969), sums up the prevailing mood of shame and cynicism among the more aware of the British and French observers. Two French officials were strolling the Munich streets at three o'clock in the morning following the agreement; Alexis Léger of the Foreign Ministry and Captain Paul Stehlin, an air attaché at the Berlin embassy: "'*Mais enfin,*" he [Stehlin] said to Léger, "*l'agrément, c'est un soulagement.*" (Anyway, this agreement is a relief.) Léger was silent for a moment. Then he said, "*Ah oui, un soulagement! Comme quand on a merdé dans sa culotte.*" (Oh yes, a relief all right! Like crapping in your pants.)'

The Waiting Game
[British/French/German: The Phoney War/ *Drôle de guerre/Sitzkrieg*]

Within a few minutes of Britain's declaration of war on Germany on Sunday, 3 September 1939, the first air raid sirens sounded. It was a false alarm. Nothing happened. And nothing much was to happen by way of hostilities between the two countries for the next eight months. The lack of action prompted a barbed comment from a US senator about a 'phony' war, an expression which was taken up on the other side of the Atlantic, though with the variant spelling of 'phoney'.

The inaction proceeded partly from British and French nerves and fear of retaliation, as well as from an outdated, if decent, notion of warfare. When several ideas for aerial raids were proposed to Sir Kingsley Wood, the Secretary of State for Air, he dismissed one of them (setting the Black Forest alight to deprive the Germans of timber) because it contravened the spirit of the Hague Convention and another (bombing munitions works at Essen, in the Ruhr) on the grounds that the target was 'private property'. The British did not suffer their first service fatality in France until three months after the declaration of war, and it would be six months before the first civilian was killed in an air raid. The only theatre where battle was joined straightaway was at sea, with the mistaken U-boat sinking of a British liner on the very day that war was declared and the intended torpedoing of a British battleship at Scapa Flow in October 1939.

For the British, the Phoney War turned a mood of anxious resolution into one of bored irritation, aggravated by shortages and emergency regulations. The blackout was a particular source of complaint because it curtailed social life, increased the risk of accident and encouraged crime. An astonishing 300,000 people passed through the courts in 1940 for failing to conform to blackout regulations. Such official requirements would have been doubly onerous for those who felt, however mistakenly, that it was a lot of fuss about nothing. Where were the bombers? What had become of the horrific predictions of hundreds of thousands of civilian casualties in the first few months of war (*see also* Chapter 10: The Popular Poster That Never Was)?

There were other names for these eight phoney months. In a dedicatory letter to Winston's son, Randolph Churchill, at the front of his novel *Put Out More Flags* (1942), Evelyn Waugh wrote: 'Here they [Waugh's characters] are in that odd, dead period before the Churchillian renaissance, which people called at the time the Great Bore War.' Churchill's own description of it was the Twilight War. The French termed it *la drôle* *de guerre* (*drôle* meaning funny, in both senses) while for the Germans it was *der Sitzkrieg* ('the sitting war').*

*A pun, of course, on the term *Blitzkrieg*, 'lightning war'.

In Adolf's Bad Books
[British: The Black List]

The philosopher Isaiah Berlin once said that the most malicious game the English could play was to speculate about who would have collaborated if the Nazis had launched a successful invasion. Counterfactual or speculative 'histories' describing such an invasion began appearing as early as August 1940, during the Battle of Britain, with the publication of *Loss of Eden*, reissued under the more uncompromising title *If Hitler Comes: A Cautionary Tale* in the following year. Since then there have been dozens of novels, films and television programmes speculating on the same subjects of Hitler's victory, British collaboration and/or resistance. That it is still a sensitive subject was shown by the anger roused by C.J. Sansom's rewriting of history to make Enoch Powell the Secretary of State for India in *Dominion* (2012), a novel which depicts not outright invasion but the creeping Nazification of Britain after Lord Halifax and not Churchill becomes Prime Minister in 1940.

The Germans also made their preparations for invasion, in book form. Part of the planning for Operation Sea Lion (*Seelöwe*) entailed the production of a guidebook to describe various aspects of British society and its institutions. As one would expect from the nation that gave birth to the Baedeker guides, the handbook was comprehensive, even covering areas like British Freemasonry or the Boy Scout Movement. Attached to this occupiers' guide was a list of 2,820 people, comprising British nationals and European exiles, who were to be arrested if the invasion succeeded.

Under the command of an SS colonel based in London, half a dozen task forces were to be deployed in principal cities like Manchester and Edinburgh to round up prominent opponents of the Nazis, among them politicians, publishers, writers and financiers. The fate of most of these detainees was apparent from the letters following their names in the list. Each entry was accompanied by a misleadingly innocuous bureaucratic abbreviation, with *Amt[er] IV* (Department 4) signifying the Gestapo and *Amt[er] VI* (Dept 6) Foreign Military Intelligence.

The blacklist was eclectic. Page 34, for example, includes Noël Coward alongside the wealthy hostess Nancy Cunard, together with the future Labour politician R.H.S. (Dick) Crossman and Sir Stafford Cripps, then Ambassador to Moscow and later to join the War Cabinet. On page 32 are the names of Churchill (Winston Spencer, *Ministerpräsident*, Westerham/Kent, Chartwell Manor, RSHA VI) and the man whom he supplanted as Prime Minister, Chamberlain ((Arthur) Neville, 18.3.69, *Politiker, ehemaliger* [former] *Ministerpräsident*, London, S.W.1, 10 Downing-Street). That the list was being compiled in May 1940 – Churchill became Prime Minister on the 10th of the month – is shown by the fact that Chamberlain's address is still given as 10 Downing Street even though he is referred to as the former PM. All of the individuals named above were, like Churchill, destined to be dealt with by the *RSHA VI*, i.e. the Foreign Intelligence branch of the *Reichssicherheitshauptamt* or Reich Security Main Office.

After the war was over, this list – the *Sonderfahndungsliste*

G.B. (Special Search List GB) – became known in tabloid-speak as the 'Black Book'. To have a place in it became a mark of distinction. Noël Coward commented: 'I remember Rebecca West, who shared the honour with me, sent me a telegram which read: "My dear – the people we should have been seen dead with."' The handbook was never used and the approximately 20,000 copies stored in a German warehouse were destroyed in a bombing raid. The Imperial War Museum in London has one of the few surviving originals in its collection (*see also* Chapter 11: Laughter in the Dark).

Chapter 3

Propaganda

The term 'propaganda' famously derives from the Latin name of a 17th-century body established by the Catholic Church 'for the propagation of the faith'. And indeed, it was with a zeal bordering on religious fervour that state propagandists in World War Two set about the task of keeping their populaces onside. Nowhere more so than in Nazi Germany; it speaks volumes that Joseph Goebbels' power base went by the name of 'Imperial Ministry for Public Enlightenment and Propaganda' – the glaring oxymoron was lost on this totalitarian regime. The club-footed, venom-filled little spinmeister of the Third Reich once noted: 'This is the secret of propaganda: those whom it is aimed at should be completely immersed in its ideas, without ever noticing that they are being immersed.'

White Power

[German: *die Arisierung*, **'Aryanisation'/**
Deutsches Ahnenerbe, **'German Ancestral Heritage']**

Before the advent of the Nazis, 'Aryan' was a fairly neutral term with linguistic and ethnographic associations. Deriving from the Sanskrit word, *arya* ('noble, of good family'), it character-ises a major language branch which is sometimes referred to as Indo-European. In the 19th century this proto-language was linked to a notional Aryan race which originally populated northern Europe. In Nazi theorising, this transmuted into an ideology which distinguished white Caucasians from all other (inferior) racial groups, and specifically from Jews. In *Mein Kampf*, Hitler asserted: 'The exact opposite of the Aryan is the Jew.'

The results of such 'Aryanisation' could be brutal but also bordered on the absurd. As early as 1935 Heinrich Himmler, the founder of the SS, set up the *Deutsches Ahnenerbe* (German Ancestral Heritage), a research group dedicated to finding the Aryan connection in everything from language to prehistoric megaliths. Expeditions were despatched to Tibet in pursuit of traces of the Aryan race, to Spain in a quest for the Holy Grail, and also to Cappadocia in Turkey, probably in search of the tomb of St Longinus, the centurion-convert whose spear pierced the side of Christ on the cross. Laborious efforts were made to 'prove' that Jesus was not Jewish but Aryan. Nazi attempts to sanctify the word mean that 'Aryan' is now a deeply suspect term. It is no coincidence that one of the largest gangs across the US prison system is a white supremacist group known as the Aryan Brotherhood.

The Versatile 'V'
[British: 'V for Victory']

It's a happy linguistic fact that the word for 'victory' in several European languages begins with a 'V'. The appropriately named Victor de Lavelye of the BBC Belgian service suggested using the letter as a symbol of resistance to the Nazis with the implication of ultimate victory over them. The idea was enthusiastically taken up by Douglas Ritchie, the Assistant Director of BBC European Broadcasts from 1941–4. Ritchie believed broadcasting could be a trigger for acts of disruption, often minor but cumulatively effective, in the occupied countries. Adopting the persona of 'Colonel Britton', Ritchie delivered brief exhortations which were introduced with four soft but ominous drumbeats standing for the morse code equivalent (three dots and a dash) of the letter V. The same sequence begins Beethoven's Fifth Symphony – or Symphony No. V – and these opening chords were played, this time by an orchestra, at the end of the broadcast. The popular belief that this famous symphonic opening signifies 'fate knocking at the door' implied that the Nazis would eventually meet their come-uppance.

As an opponent of tyranny, Beethoven famously removed the dedication to Napoleon from his Third Symphony but the irony that a German genius was providing stirring propaganda for the Allies in the early stages of World War Two cannot have been lost on either side. The Germans tried to appropriate the V-for-victory campaign also by using Beethoven's Fifth. On the Eiffel Tower in occupied Paris was installed a vast 'V' with the legend underneath DEUTSCHLAND SIEGT AUF ALLEN FRONTEN ('Germany is victorious on all fronts'). But the letter/sign was always more fittingly identified with opposition to the Nazis. In the German-occupied Netherlands, the resis-tance took to daubing the 'V' sign on walls overnight as an act of defiance, and under it the legend 'OZO'. These letters were short for *Oranje zal Overwinnen* ('Orange [i.e. the House of Orange, the Dutch royal family] Will Triumph'). Another, more sinister, acronym that gained currency after the invasion was HALLO; ostensibly the innocuous Dutch word for 'Hello', in this guise it stood for *Hang Alle Laffe Landverraders Op* – 'String Up All Cowardly Traitors' a reference to the hated

Nationaal-Socialistische Beweging (NSB), the homegrown Nazis who had actively collaborated in the German seizure of their country. The widespread Allied use of the 'V' was finally vindicated, as it were, by the celebration of V-E Day (Victory in Europe) on 8 May 1945 and V-J Day (Victory in Japan) on 15 August 1945.

Winston Churchill always stressed the need for victory rather than mere survival and, in a broadcast to Europe in July 1941, soon after the V-campaign was launched by the BBC, he said:

> *The V sign is the symbol of the unconquerable will of the occupied territories and a portent of the fate awaiting Nazi tyranny.*

Around this time Churchill began using the V-sign as a trademark gesture. Some early photos show him doing it the 'wrong' way round, i.e. not with the palm outwards but with the back of the hand facing onlookers, then (as now) an obscene gesture. His private secretary noted his habit of doing it despite being repeatedly told that 'this gesture has quite another significance'. Churchill must have got the message eventually because most later pictures show him making the right sort of V-sign.

Lure of the Crooked Cross

[German: *das Hakenkreuz,* 'swastika'**]**

The swastika, the most recognisable and widespread symbol of German National Socialism, is one of the most effective pieces of political branding ever devised. Even now, almost seventy years after the end of World War Two, it still has the power to enrage and disgust whenever we see footage of it sprayed by neo-Nazis on desecrated Jewish cemeteries.

It is well known that the swastika goes far back beyond the NSDAP's misuse of it as the *Hakenkreuz* (literally 'hook cross'). The English term, from the Sanskrit *svastika*, points to its origins in the ancient Indus Valley Civilisations at the settlements of Harappa and Mohenjo-Daro. The word is composed of elements meaning 'good, well' and the verbal root 'to be,' along with the diminutive element '-*ka*'; the whole word thus roughly translates as 'little thing associated with good/well-being' – a profoundly ironic etymology, given its most infamous historical manifestation.

The precise origin of the English term 'the crooked cross' for the swastika is unclear. It was clearly common currency by 1940, when a churchman, Dr A. S. Duncan-Jones, Dean of Chichester Cathedral, wrote an essay with this title for the *Macmillan War Pamphlets* series. The image encapsulates the main theme of the writer's thesis: that Nazism is a form of religion, yet is at total variance with the values of Christianity ('*The secret of the success of National Socialism lies precisely in the religious, mystical element, symbolised in the Swastika*'). The pejorative undertone of the alliterative phrase couldn't be plainer: a grotesque parody, a sick perversion of the true faith.

Yet divested of its negative 20th-century Western connotations, the swastika is still widely displayed in Hindu, Buddhist and Jainist cultures as a good-luck charm. Somewhat odder at first sight is its use in Finland; it made its first widespread appearance during the country's brief civil war of 1918, as a good-fortune symbol taken from the family crest of the White (Conservative) Army supporter and Swedish nobleman Count

Eric von Rosen. A keen aviator, Rosen donated an aircraft to the Whites, and emblazoned it with the swastika, in blue on a white circular background. This remained the official insignia of the Finnish Air Force until 1945, and though the fuselage identification was changed thereafter to a blue-and-white roundel, the swastika persists to this day on officers' epaulettes and regional air-force command flags as well as on some Finnish medals and decorations. Rosen apparently first saw the symbol on Viking graves on the island of Gotland; perhaps these legendarily long-distance travellers encountered it on their raids, or it may have had a separate Nordic mythological origin. In any event, Finns are very keen to dissociate their use of the swastika from any taint of Nazism – though Rosen was a member of the National Socialist Bloc, an aristocratic Swedish party, and in a strange twist of fate later became *Luftwaffe* commander Hermann Goering's brother-in-law.

The upsurge of interest in all things mystical and folkloristic in the early years of the 20th century brought the swastika to greater public consciousness. Some commentators trace awareness of the symbol to archaeologist Heinrich Schliemann's discovery of this form of decoration in his much-publicised excavation of the ancient city of Troy. And so the crooked cross crops up in all sorts of innocuous contexts after the turn of the century. In 1907, a claim was staked in northern Ontario for the Swastika Gold Mine, presumably so-named because a slice of good luck is just what you need when prospecting for gold. The town that grew up nearby styled itself Swastika, a name it has clung onto steadfastly ever since, despite the best efforts of an embarrassed Canadian provincial government to change it – notably in World War Two, to 'Winston'. (In the second twist of fate in this story

– this time even more bizarre – the British Union of Fascists' supporter Lord Redesdale soon acquired control of the Swastika mine and his daughter Unity Mitford, whom Hitler praised as 'a perfect specimen of Aryan womanhood', was allegedly conceived in the town in 1914.) Also in Canada, an ice hockey team, which played for eleven years in a local amateur league in Nova Scotia from 1905–16, went by the name of the 'Windsor Swastikas' – not to be confused with Prince Harry's unfortunate choice of fancy dress costume exactly a century later.

Likewise, in 1910, a picture-postcard mailed from Rochester, NY to a recipient in Connecticut – and recently offered for sale on eBay – indicates how well embedded the symbol must have been in the popular imagination by that time. Beside a large depiction of the symbol is the ditty:

> *In ancient days Swastika*
> *Possessed a magic charm*
> *And shielded its possessor*
> *From danger and from harm*
>
> *To you it brings Good Wishes*
> *And if I had the power*
> *'Twould bring you all that life holds dear*
> *This very day and hour*

Two years later, in 1912, the 'Swastika Laundry' was founded in the Ballsbridge suburb of Dublin by John W. Brittain (evidently a fan of the symbol; he also owned a racehorse named 'Swastika Rose'). Plying its trade around the Irish capital in electric-powered pillarbox-red vans sporting a large black swastika on a white background, in 1939 the firm took to clearly advertising the date of its establishment on its vehicles, to avoid any unwanted associations with the by-then more notorious users of the image.* Even so, the sight of one of these vans was enough to unnerve German Nobel Prize-winning author Heinrich Böll when he lived in Ireland for a spell in the 1950s. In his *Irish Diary*, Böll described a close shave with a Swastika Laundry van:

> *Had someone sold Völkischer Beobachter [the National Socialist party newspaper] delivery trucks here, or did the Völkischer Beobachter still have a branch office here? This one looked exactly like those I remembered; but the driver crossed himself as he smilingly signalled to me to proceed, and on closer inspection I saw what had happened. It was simply the 'Swastika Laundry' which had painted the year of its founding, 1912, clearly beneath the swastika . . .*

But also in the 1910s, those of a nationalistic, anti-Semitic disposition, such as the Austrian poet and journalist Guido von List (1848–1919) began to identify specious ethnographic significance in the swastika. List popularised it as a sun-cross rune from an 'Aryan race' with its fountainhead in northern India, which according to *völkisch* and later Nazi ideology was the seedbed of the Nordic peoples who had gone on to gain mastery over the Earth. The occultist oddball, List, was responsible for giving the German language the term *Hakenkreuz*.

When the demobbed corporal Adolf Hitler embarked on his career of demagoguery, he quickly co-opted the swastika as the ideal symbol for his own movement, which formally adopted it in 1920. Prior to this, it had been used by right-wing militias such as the Erhardt Brigade of the *Freikorps* militias which brutally overthrew the workers' republics proclaimed in Berlin and Munich in 1919 (they sang the marching-song: '*Hakenkreuz am Stahlhelm, Schwarz-weiß-rotes Band, Die Brigade Ehrhardt Werden wir genannt.*' 'Swastika on helmets/Colours red-white-black/The Brigade Erhardt/Is marching to attack'). Hitler explained his rationale in *Mein Kampf*:

In the swastika [we see embodied] the mission of the struggle for the victory of the Aryan man and by the same virtue the victory of the idea of creative work, which as such always has been and always will be anti-Semitic.

But for all his pseudo-anthropological theorising, Hitler well understood the power of the visual image, especially one with as much graphic impact as this. Again in *Mein Kampf*, he describes his deliberations on the appearance of the party banner (which was made the official flag of the Third Reich on 15 September 1935). His words would not be out of place in the mouth of a creative director of an advertising agency:

Around that time, I was greatly preoccupied with the question of the party flag, namely the way it should look. For the new flag had to be both a symbol of our own struggle and have a striking, poster-like impact. Anyone who has had any extensive dealings with the masses will know that such apparent trivialities really matter. A truly effective symbol can, in many hundreds of thousands of cases, be the first impetus towards a person taking an interest in a political movement.

We can fairly assume that the Führer's choice of colours for his new flag did not take its inspiration from the Ballsbridge laundry. Rather, the red, white and black harked back to the flags of the Prussian-led North German Confederation (1867) and thereafter the Second Empire (1871) – a neat trick for suggesting the historical continuity of a totalitarian regime that far surpassed its predecessors in dispensing with any constitutional checks and balances.

Following Hitler's accession to the German Chancellorship in 1933, in the lead-up to World War Two and during the conflict, the symbol was ubiquitous in Germany and in annexed Austria and other regions: proudly displayed on the armbands of Hitler Youth members, or on the vast vertical banners hung above the podium at the Nuremberg rallies, and at the other end of the scale reproduced in tiny form in the centre of the Iron Cross award for gallantry in the field. As befitted a totalitarian regime, the Nazis guarded the use of the swastika and related symbols every bit as jealously as the McDonald's Corporation protects its Golden Arches corporate logo. Joseph Goebbels's Ministry for Public Enlightenment and Propaganda issued directives listing the permitted uses of this 'sovereign symbol of the new state': New Year's greeting cards and Christmas tree decorations with the swastika were allowed, but wooden menu-card holders and jumpers with swastika appliqués were *verboten*.

Of course, the symbol's graphic power also made it a gift for those who hated Nazism and all its works. During the Weimar Republic and even after the NSDAP's ascent to power, the satirical artist John Heartfield (real name Helmut Herzfeld: 1891–1968) produced numerous posters warning of Nazism's brutality. One from 1934 (entitled 'Blood and Iron') shows four axes, looking remarkably like the one in the lictor's bundle that Mussolini's fascists took as their symbol, arranged in a swastika shape and dripping blood. Another of his works, from the same year, has a medieval image of a heretic broken on a wheel set above a collage of a man being agonisingly crucified on the crooked cross; the two-part legend runs: 'As in the Middle Ages . . . So in the Third Reich.' Many political cartoonists followed Heartfield in lampooning the Nazi's 'symbol of sovereignty'.

Along with other Nazi insignia, the swastika was outlawed when Hitler's Thousand-Year Reich came to its predictably cataclysmic end 988 years prematurely, in May 1945. Paragraph 86a of the German Federal Criminal Code states that portrayals of the swastika in modern Germany are permissible only in the service of 'public enlightenment, in resisting attempts to undermine the constitution, for artistic, scientific, research or teaching purposes, or for documenting current affairs or historical events or to any similar such ends'. Images of National Socialist memorabilia offered for sale on German auction websites still have to have the swastikas obscured, however vestigially.

The British humourist Alan Coren found out about Federal Germany's fear and loathing of the swastika the hard way. In 1975, he compiled a collection of his essays for *Punch* magazine and released them in book form under the title *Golfing for Cats*; its dust jacket displayed a large swastika. Coren's logic was impeccable – he'd scanned the bestseller lists and found that titles on golf, felines and the Third Reich consistently sold well. So why not combine all three, and slap it on the cover of a book that had nothing whatsoever to do with any of those subjects? He had reckoned, however, without the diligent efficiency of the German police, who swooped on his publisher's stand at that year's Frankfurt Book Fair and impounded every last copy. Then again, all publicity is grist to the satirist's mill.

*The company ceased trading in the 1960s but was bought out by another concern that operated from the same premises, using the same name and logo, until the late 1980s. The laundry chimney is still standing, though it has been purged of the white swastikas and the large vertical letters spelling 'Swastika Laundry' that once adorned it.

Lauding the Duce

[Italian: *Giovinezza*, 'Youth' (title of the Fascist anthem)/*Eja, Eja, alalà!*, 'Hip, hip, hooray!']

Just like the *Horst Wessel Lied* in Nazi Germany (*see* Chapter 13: Paean to a Pimp), Fascist Italy also had its own 'unofficial' national anthem. Entitled *Giovinezza* ('Youth'), the tune actually predates Mussolini's rise to power. It was written in 1909 by a composer called Giovanni Blanc, under the name *Il Commiato* ('The Farewell'), and in this first incarnation was a students' song, popular among graduates of the University of Turin. Its original lyrics recalled the halcyon days of a carefree student life now past, and celebrated strength, youth and beauty. *Il Commiato* was then taken up as a stirring marching song in World War One, becoming a particular favourite of the *Arditi*, the élite corps of the Italian Army, many of whom were to join the Fascist cause after the war and form the core of its shock-troops, the *Squadristi* (Blackshirts). It was also sung at the mass rallies staged in 1919 by the writer, war hero and proto-Fascist political agitator Gabriele D'Annunzio in the disputed seaport of Fiume (now Rijeka, Croatia), which the Irredentist movement claimed for Italy.

It is a measure of the tune's popularity that in 1924, two

years after he took power, Mussolini personally commissioned a new set of verses, by Salvator Gotta, and restyled it as the 'triumphal hymn of the National Fascist Party'. Along with references to warriors, heroes and the Fatherland, the song now included paeans of praise to the *Duce* himself. For instance, the fourth stanza ran: *E per Benito Mussolini/Eja, Eja, Alalà!/E per la nostra patria bella/Eja, Eja, Alalà!* ('And for Benito Mussolini/Hip, hip, hooray!/And for our beautiful fatherland/Hip, hip, hooray!') The strange exclamation repeated in this verse was the invention of D'Annunzio, and derived from his war service as an aviator.

D'Annunzio had been fascinated by aviation since 1908. When war broke out, he enlisted and, despite being unable to fly, was given command of a squadron. In 1917, he led three bombing raids on Pola (Pula in Croatia), the principal Austrian naval base on the Adriatic. Before the last of these, which took place on 8–9 August and involved 36 aircraft, he inspired his San Marco Squadron with the rousing cry *Eja! Eja! Eja! Alalà!* In characteristically florid style, D'Annunzio subsequently described the elation the Italian fliers felt after completing their mission:

> *The alalà was inaugurated at the summit of the most beautiful youthful virtue . . . On the way home it seemed to us as if we had conquered all the stars for Italy.*

The author had long been searching for an equivalent of 'hip, hip, hooray' (which was hard for Italians to say and anyhow, being of Saxon origin, was considered 'barbaric' by the self-styled aesthete and aristocrat). Finally, he 'discovered the primitive cry of my race' in what he claimed was the chant that Achilles had once used to spur his horses into battle (Alala was the daughter of Polemos, the god of war). D'Annunzio's war cry stuck and became the vocal counterpart of the straight-armed Roman salute in the Fascist era.

As for *Giovinezza*, conductor Arturo Toscanini's steadfast refusal to play it before operas at La Scala and elsewhere brought him into conflict with the regime and its supporters. In 1931 in Bologna, he was jostled and assaulted by a gang of Fascist thugs, and never returned to Italy for the duration of the war. Having been so strongly associated with the discredited totalitarian regime, the anthem was outlawed after 1945, and the singing of it remains banned to this day.

Workers' Playtime, German Style
[German: *Kraft durch Freude*, 'Strength through Joy']

When the Nazis came to power, they lost no time in outlawing both trades unions and employers' organisations; the old antagonism of proletariat vs plutocracy was to be swept away in a radical reformation of German industry and commerce. The single organisation to supplant this class-based system, the *Deutsche Arbeitsfront* (*DAF*; German Labour Front), came into being in early May 1933 and for the entire duration of the Third Reich was headed by Dr Robert Ley. For his complicity in the conscription and maltreatment of wartime slave labour, Ley was indicted at the Nuremberg war crimes trials but hanged himself before sentence could be passed.

The most famous aspect of the Labour Front was the pompously entitled 'Strength Through Joy' (*Kraft durch Freude*; abbreviated to *KdF*) programme, which was dedicated to offering leisure activities to the country's workforce. Theatre trips, concerts and art exhibitions were laid on. Mass guided walking holidays were organised and workers were also given the hitherto unimaginable opportunity to go on cruises to Norway, Madeira or Italy on single-class ocean liners, some of them newly constructed; the pride of the *KdF* fleet were the 25,000+-ton vessels *MS Wilhelm Gustloff* (*see* Chapter 11: Cooper's Snoopers and the Nun with the Stubble) and the MS *Robert Ley*. Another scheme was for huge beach resorts where 20,000 people could holiday at a time. Six were planned, but only one built – the so-called 'Colossus of Prora' on the Baltic island of Rügen, a massive 4.5-kilometre-long complex of eight apartment blocks, where every room had a sea view. This Butlins on steroids was never used for its intended purpose, being completed only just before the outbreak of war.

It is in the nature of totalitarian states to stretch their tentacles into every corner of the individual's life, so the stated aim of the programme was not just to provide recreation but also to imbue workers with the ideals of National Socialism and convince them of its communitarian beneficence. In Nazi Germany, even after clocking off, your time was not your own – a key concept of the *KdF* programme was *Feierabendgestaltung* ('leisure-time structuring', an oxymoron to modern ears). A 1939 publication on the organisation made clear its agenda:

The full scope of the work and the goals of the National Socialist 'Strength through Joy' association can only be properly understood and appreciated if one views them not in isolation, but rather constantly reminds oneself that they form an indispensable part of the total political programme of the New State.

One major initiative to boost employment and give workers new mobility was the plan to manufacture a mass-produced, affordable and robust family saloon. This was the genesis of the *KdF-Wagen* ('Strength Through Joy Car'), the Volkswagen Beetle. Designed by Ferdinand Porsche, it was to be assembled at a purpose-built plant in a new town imaginatively called *Stadt des KdF-Wagens* (later renamed Wolfsburg, in Lower Saxony). Like Prora, this was another scheme that fell foul of the war; no Beetles found their way to ordinary buyers before the factory was turned over to production of the *Kübelwagen* ('bucket car'), the German equivalent of the Jeep.

English Pastoral

[British: *'Went the Day Well?'* – title of a 1942 propaganda film]

The camera wobbles towards a country signpost. To the right and at a distance of 6½ miles is UPTON FERRARS, while to the left, only a quarter of a mile off, is the village of BRAMLEY END. The camera veers down a country lane until it reaches a scatter of houses before settling on a cottage next to a churchyard. A local – cloth-capped and pipe-smoking – is sitting outside with his dog. He gets to his feet and speaks directly to the camera: 'Good day to you. Come to have a look at Bramley End, have you?'

As he wanders towards the graveyard he tells us that we aren't really here to appreciate the peace of the village or the picturesque 13th-century church but to hear about the battle of Bramley End. Gesturing with his pipe, he points to a new memorial surmounted by a large cross. The names inscribed on it are German: 'They wanted England, these Jerries did. And this is the only bit they got.'

So begins one of the most effective and dramatic British films of the war years. *Went the Day Well?* (the title comes from a poetic epitaph of World War One) had a distinguished pedigree. With music by William Walton and a script by Graham Greene from one of his own short stories, it shows a band of German paratroopers disguised as British soldiers taking over an idyllic village in preparation for a full-scale invasion. The drama isn't confined to the gradual realisation by the villagers that the enemy is in their midst. The revelation, shown early on to the cinema audience, that the village squire is a Fifth Columnist (*see* Chapter 11: Cooper's Snoopers and the Nun with the Stubble) still has the power to surprise, even shock. So, too, does the violence with which the villagers eventually meet the violence of their would-be occupiers. It's as if Miss Marple were to get out her knitting needle and dispatch the murderer herself.

It ends happily, of course. The framing device using the old cloth-capped rustic with his dog has already informed us of that from the beginning. This is a story only to be told, he says, 'after the war was over and old Hitler got what was coming to him', a more confident and bold statement in 1942 when the film was made than it would have been three years earlier.

Part of the impact of *Went the Day Well?* derives from the contrast between the village of Bramley End* and the small-scale version of the fighting which erupts in these innocent, bucolic surroundings. But the idyllic May landscape – the film was shot in a Chilterns village – with its birdsong, its hills and hedgerows and its close-knit community was an implicit reminder to the audience that this is exactly what they were fighting for, the right to go on living undisturbed in a peaceful and pastoral setting.

39

Inevitably, the war prompted a wave of jingoistic propaganda and exhortations from government and organisations such as the BBC. But there were quieter, more subtle forms of patriotism, understated praise of the British character and celebrations of Englishness. Collections of prose and pictures reminded people of the glories of the countryside. A series of four soft propaganda posters distributed by the Army Bureau of Current Affairs in 1942 showed pictures of a village green, a country fair, Salisbury Cathedral and the South Downs with a shepherd and his dog in the foreground, all accompanied with the legend: 'Your BRITAIN. Fight for it now.'

Evelyn Waugh's novel *Brideshead Revisited* (1945) is one of the lushest pastoral evocations of them all. Waugh later came to regard it with some distaste, explaining away its luxuriance by saying that it was born of 'a bleak period of present privation and threatening disaster'. At the beginning of the novel, Charles Ryder, narrator, artist and now army officer, finds himself in the middle of the war billeted at Brideshead, the great country house where he was introduced to the aristocratic Marchmain family:

'I have been here before,' I said; I had been there before; first with Sebastian more than twenty years ago on a cloudless day in June, when the ditches were white with fools' parsley and meadowsweet and the air heavy with all the scents of summer; it was a day of peculiar splendour, such as our climate affords once or twice in the year, when leaf and flower and bird and sun-lit stone and shadow seem all to proclaim the glory of God; and though I had been there so often, in so many moods, it was to that first visit that my heart returned on this, my latest.

Among other things, *Brideshead Revisited* is an example of linguistic compensation, of the way in which stately language could remind readers of an idealised England.

*The Buckinghamshire village of Turville acted the part of Bramley End. The picturesqueness of the real-life village and its proximity to film studios past and present like Pinewood and Ealing mean that Turville and the nearby village of Hambleden have frequently been used as film and TV locations. (Turville's credits also include *The Vicar of Dibley, An Education* and *Midsomer Murders*.)

Pact of Steel
[British/American: Axis]

The political alliance between Germany and Italy gave fresh life to 'axis'. This old synonym for 'pivot' was not much used outside astronomical circles, having largely been supplanted by 'axle', before it appeared in a new guise in a newspaper article of 1936. *The Times* commented that '*The "Rome–Berlin axis", is a conceit which has its momentary attractions*'.* A political treaty signed in 1936 became three years later a military alliance (to which Mussolini gave the name Pact of Steel or *Patto d'Acciaio*). In theory at least, the Axis, the common pivot on which Germany and Italy spun together, was stronger than ever with the outbreak of war. In 1940 the Axis was extended to the Far East, with the signing of the Tripartite Pact between the two European fascist states and Japan. Other countries sometimes included among the list of Axis powers were Romania, Bulgaria and Hungary.

The term produced a number of spin-offs such as 'axis forces' and even a villainess in the shape of 'Axis Sally', an American woman who broadcast pro-German propaganda. There were occasional attempts to make the term apply to the Allied side ('*The London–Washington Axis*') but in general it was used only about the Nazis and their allies. It was a common term in reports, propaganda and publicity campaigns of all kinds: a US poster aimed at its own armed services says: 'You can't beat the Axis if you get VD.'

It's not hard to see why the term appealed to the opponents of Nazism. 'Axis' has a harsher sound than 'alliance', while stressing the mechanistic rather than the human quality of the enemy. In addition, there may be some half-conscious association with the axe-imagery which was so prominent a part of Italian fascist paraphernalia.

The World War Two context was deliberately echoed by President George W. Bush in his State of the Union address to Congress in January 2002, following the attacks of 9/11. Talking of the 'Axis of Evil', he linked three countries, Iran, Iraq and North Korea, for their authoritarian leadership and aggressive stance towards the outside world. The Iraq invasion followed shortly afterwards. The parallels with the original Axis were dubious. Iraq and Iran were never allies, unlike Germany and Italy, and they had fought a bitter and bloody war in the 1980s, while North Korea seemed to have been thrown into the mix to make up the numbers of rogue states.

*This *Times* article of 3 November 1936 was referring to a speech delivered to a huge crowd outside Milan Cathedral by Mussolini two days earlier, in which he had coined the term 'axis' in this new political sense: 'This Berlin–Rome vertical line is not an obstacle but rather an axis [*Asse*] around which can revolve all those European states with a will to collaboration and peace.'

Propaganda

The Grandeur That Was Rome

[Italian: *Romanità/Natale di Roma*, 'Roman-ness'/
'Birth of Rome', a Fascist bank holiday]

The Italian Fascists were adept at having their ideological cake and eating it, too. On the one hand, as the self-proclaimed shock troops of a new, forward-looking Italy, they eagerly espoused many aspects of modernism. The futurist *enfant terrible* and purveyor of Fascist agitprop, Filippo Tommaso Marinetti, famously lauded speed and dynamism and called for the abolition of pasta, as the stodgy fare of an outmoded age ('Spaghetti is no food for fighters. In the conflict to come the victory will be to the swift!'). But on the other hand, they were all too keen to associate their programme of national renewal with the *imperium* of ancient Rome.

In fact, the concept known as *Romanità* (Latin: *Romanitas*, 'Roman-ness') lay at the very heart of Mussolini's agenda. Fascism constantly harked back to the halcyon days of the Roman Empire. The central symbol that gave the movement its name, the lictor's bundle of rods, or *fasces*, derived from that period (*see* Chapter 12: Enemy Aliens). Also, one of the first acts of the new regime when it took power in 1922 was to institute a public holiday on 21 April celebrating the *Natale di Roma* – the birth of Rome – as a Fascist day of labour to replace the socialist May Day. On that very day, in the newspaper *Il Popolo d'Italia* which he had founded eight years before, Mussolini wrote a leader entitled 'The Past and the Future', in which he proclaimed: 'Rome is our guiding star; it is our symbol – or if you prefer, our myth.'

The *Duce*'s invasion of Abyssinia in 1935 was a conscious attempt to revive Rome's African empire. The campaign was

43

marked in equal measure by incompetence and barbarism (notably the use of poison gas). Two years later and Mussolini, whom American war correspondent William L. Shirer dubbed a 'strutting, sawdust Roman Caesar', was clearly inviting comparison with Augustus when he opened the 'Augustan Exhibition of Roman-ness' (*Mostra Augustea della Romanità*) on 23 September 1937, to commemorate the two-thousandth anniversary of the birth of the first emperor.

Ancient and modern came together in the grand construction project for the *Esposizione Universale di Roma* (E.U.R.), the World's Fair, due to be held in Rome in 1942 but cancelled because of the outbreak of war. The main building work went ahead anyway, producing a White City of sterile, forbidding structures in the neoclassical modernist idiom. E.U.R. conveys nothing of the intended grandeur of a new imperial capital, being more reminiscent of the cold and depopulated cityscapes seen in the nightmarish work of the surrealist painter Giorgio de Chirico.

Chapter 4

Wartime Speeches

On 9 April 1963, in the Rose Garden of the White House, President John F. Kennedy presided over a ceremony awarding honorary US citizenship to Winston Churchill, one of only two occasions on which honorary American citizenship has been offered to a living individual. At the age of 89, Churchill watched the ceremony by satellite relay while sitting in his London home. In what is perhaps the best-known section of his speech, the President said of Churchill: 'In the dark days and darker nights when Britain stood alone – and most men save Englishmen despaired of England's life – he mobilised the English language and sent it into battle.' In the 1940s the leaders of the warring nations were able to speak directly to their people either at mass rallies, as in Nuremberg, or through the radio. For the first time, their words were heard by millions.

Finest Hours
[Churchill's mobilisation of language]

Winston Churchill's BBC broadcasts during World War Two were his principal channel to the British people and to other nations. While the man himself was glimpsed by many during his Blitz walkabouts and troop inspections, and many more read the speeches he delivered in parliament, it was only through the medium of radio that his voice could be heard by millions. The signal was not so clear or powerful in those days and listeners were forced to cluster round the set, probably the only one in the house, fiddling with the dial in order to separate the voice from the background static. Then out of the wireless would emerge the sound of the man who was not only the military and political leader of the nation but, in a sense, the very embodiment of it.

Churchill's words were carefully selected to serve several purposes. The most significant was to keep up the morale of the British and to mobilise the entire population, especially the great civilian majority. This universal involvement was one of the things that made the conflict different from World War One since, as Churchill said, the 'fronts are everywhere'. At the same time he had to look beyond Britain itself. He had to convey hope and a sense of solidarity with the occupied countries of Europe. He had to show defiance to the enemy while making tactful references to the role which he believed the United States would eventually play in the fighting. He needed to fit the speech to the occasion: reassurance and resilience when times were bad; caution and restraint at moments of triumph. Churchill required a style which was distinct from – more elevated than – everyday speech, but not one which was so refined and abstract that it left his listeners unmoved or confused about his meaning.

The rhythm and phrasing of the speeches which resulted, or at least the more famous ones, owe something to the Bible, to the Elizabethans, to historical stylists such as Gibbon and Macaulay whom Churchill pored over for instruction when he was young. In his words at the outbreak of World War Two is detectable the spirit of Queen Elizabeth's speech to her troops at the port of Tilbury in 1588, the year of the Spanish Armada ('I . . . think it foul scorn that Palma or Spain, or any prince of Europe, should dare invade the borders of my realm . . .'). In their exhortation and sense of historical destiny, there are links with the language Shakespeare gives to Henry V on the eve of Agincourt, the anniversary of which, declares the king, will never pass 'From this day to the ending of the world,/But we in it shall be remembered,/We few, we happy few, we band of brothers.' Winston Churchill was surely recalling this piece of Shakespeare in his famous tribute to the young pilots of the RAF: 'Never was so much owed by so many to so few.' It's no coincidence that later in the war, the government that he led encouraged Laurence Olivier to make a film of *Henry V*. This story of a victorious and historic English invasion of France was released at the end of 1944, when enough time had elapsed for the D-Day landings to have become an irreversible success.

Perhaps no moment of the war was as threatening as that following the French surrender and the early stages of the Battle of Britain, when it seemed as though the Germans planned to knock out the RAF before mounting an invasion. In a broadcast made on 14 July 1940, Churchill talked with feeling of the defeat of France and looked forward to the eventual liberation of that country, before going on:

We are fighting by ourselves alone; but we are not fighting for ourselves alone. Here in this strong City of Refuge which enshrines the title-deeds of human progress and is of deep consequence to Christian civilisation; here, girt about by the seas and oceans where the Navy reigns; shielded from above by the prowess and devotion of our

airmen – we await undismayed the impending assault.
Perhaps it will come tonight. Perhaps it will come next
week. Perhaps it will never come.

There are familiar rhetorical devices here, mostly involving
repetition with variation (the second half of the first sentence
duplicates the first with the difference of a single word: 'for'
instead of 'by'). The choice of language, while not obscure, is
not found in everyday speech ('title deeds of civilisation', 'of
deep consequence', 'the Navy reigns'). The sentences are
of contrasting lengths: one long one beginning 'Here', and
then three short ones starting with 'Perhaps'. The phrase 'city
of refuge' comes from the Old Testament. The description of
Britain as 'girt about by the seas' recalls the famous
Shakespearean speech in *Richard II* about 'This precious
stone set in a silver sea', while the the lines about the imminent invasion sound like an echo – deliberate or otherwise
– of a passage from *Hamlet* to do with death and readiness
('If it be now, 'tis not to come; if it be not to come, it will
be now . . .').

The delivery was enormously important. Churchill spoke in
conventional upper-class, educated tones, like almost all the
'official' voices heard on the BBC at the time. He took as much
care as an actor over the scripts of his speeches, with the
difference that these were scripts he had written himself.
And, like an actor, he knew when to pause or speed up for
effect, when to raise or lower his voice for emphasis. Pauses
were especially important and if, as an experiment, a broadcast speech is edited to do away with them, then a lot of the
effect is lost. Given the impact of the speeches, it is interesting
to note that Churchill did not enjoy broadcasting. A born

performer, he needed an audience in front of him, or at his feet, such as he enjoyed in the House of Commons. For all that, his listeners responded as he must have wanted. One wrote that his words 'sent shivers (not of fear) down my spine'. People felt elevated to the level of his rhetoric. In their more buoyant moods they could even catch sight of those 'broad sunlit uplands' which he promised for the world when the war was won.

One of the strengths of Churchill's broadcasts was that he could be matter-of-fact since he believed that 'our people do not mind being told the worst'. A speech of 18 June 1940 begins simply 'The news from France is very bad' even if it ends with the rousing call-to-arms 'This was their finest hour' (again reminiscent of *Henry V*). The famously blunt and ominous comment by the Prime Minister about all he could offer being 'blood, toil, tears and sweat', though made in the first place to parliament, soon rang round the country once it was reported by the BBC.

It wasn't all resonant phrase-making, though. When he was addressing the House of Commons rather than the country, he could afford to let a dry humour show. The worst fears of the effect of Luftwaffe bombing were not fulfilled, and early civilian casualties in the Blitz were less than a tenth of the figures expected. So it may have been relief as well as mischief that prompted Churchill to say to the House in October 1940: 'Statisticians may amuse themselves by calculating that after making allowance for the working of the law of diminishing returns, through the same house being struck twice or three times over, it would take 10 years at the present rate, for half the houses of London to be demolished. After that, of course, progress would be much slower.' In the same speech Churchill makes an encouraging point about the effectiveness of bomb shelters but that doesn't stop him from coming up with another, rather macabre, deadpan calculation: 'On that particular Thursday night 180 persons were killed in London as a result of 251 tons of bombs. That is to say, it took one ton of bombs to kill three-quarters of a person.'

The more typical orator is to be found in remarks he made to parliament and also broadcast the day after the German surrender in 1945. Churchill concedes that 'a brief period of rejoicing' is allowed before reminding his audience that Japan still has to be defeated: 'We must now devote all our strength and resources to the completion of our task, both at home and abroad. Advance, Britannia! Long live the cause of freedom! God save the King!' In the cry, like that of a knight riding out to battle, is a combination of romanticism, chivalry and patriotism* – curiously archaic, closer to fiction than reality, almost certainly unrepeatable, but perfectly fitted to the moment.

*It's no coincidence that, in his famous 'We shall fight on the beaches' speech of June 1940 shortly after he became Prime Minister, Churchill should have gone to Alfred Tennyson's 19th-century poem *Morte D'Arthur* when he wanted an analogy for the bravery of the young pilots who would soon be fighting in the Battle of Britain:

> *Every morn brought forth a noble chance,*
> *And every chance brought forth a noble knight.*

Revealingly, Churchill made the two lines even more archaic than they were in the original. Tennyson actually wrote '*When every morning brought a noble chance,/And every chance brought out a noble knight.*'

A Pernicious Rumour

[The Winston 'impersonator']

An odd footnote to the story of Winston Churchill's speeches is the rumour, which has circulated for many years, that some of his broadcasts were actually made by the actor Norman Shelley (1903–80). Shelley enjoyed a long career on the radio, playing Dennis the Dachshund in the children's series *Toytown* and Dr Watson in Sherlock Holmes dramatisations back in the 1950s. He had a rich voice, which to a later age sounds distinctly actorly and even fruity. He also had a high opinion of himself as a Churchill impersonator. It may be true that Shelley did record at least one of Churchill's speeches – the famously defiant 'We shall fight on the beaches' is often mentioned – but, if so, it was for commercial purposes and with Churchill's agreement or at least his acquiescence. There is no convincing evidence that Shelley made any of the radio broadcasts.

Why would Churchill have required an impersonator in any case? The usual answer is that he was too busy to make the broadcasts himself or – a more damaging claim – that he was too drunk to do so. But the significant and interesting question is: where does the story come from? The clue as to why the rumour exists in the first place is provided by the identity of the person who started it. David Irving, the extreme right-wing historian, claimed in *Churchill's War* (1987) to have heard the story from Norman Shelley himself. But Irving had an axe to grind, and diminishing Churchill's near-mythic status was part of his purpose. As the historian Robert Rhodes James points out, such a dramatic claim from such a source ought to have been treated with suspicion. Yet the Shelley-impersonation tale was picked up by a number of writers and journalists even though some of Irving's factual assertions were questionable: for example, he claimed to have interviewed Norman Shelley more than a year after the actor had died. In Rhodes James's words, these insinuations about the wartime broadcasts may be dismissed as 'part of the ugly tapestry of denigration of Churchill' begun by revisionist historians such as Irving.

Style over Substance

[Hitler's demagogic oratory]

In 1936, for one of his five contributions to an illustrated book of essays on Adolf Hitler, Nazi Propaganda Minister Joseph Goebbels wrote a brief, but suitably fawning, appraisal of his leader's gift of the gab. Lauding Hitler in quasi-religious terms as a 'proclaimer of the Word' and placing him in a pantheon of speakers which included Caesar, Frederick the Great and Bismarck, Goebbels, no mean rabble-rouser himself, claimed:

Hitler's 'leadership of the masses' is so unique and extraordinary that it fits no standard template or dogma. It would be absurd to imagine that he had attended some school of oratory or speech training; he is a rhetorical genius who has emerged with no external influence, conscious or otherwise.

(Der Führer als Redner/'The Führer as Orator')

Fittingly, this was pure propaganda on Goebbels' part; Hitler's mature public speaking style was no innate gift, but the result of careful tuition. In 1932, fearing that his vocal cords might become paralysed through overuse, Hitler sought the help of an operatic tenor called Paul Devrient. In his diary, published in 1975 as *Mein Schüler Hitler* ('My Pupil Hitler'), the singer revealed that, as well as teaching the Führer voice-training techniques, he also schooled him in gesture, facial expression and posture. These visits were, of course, hushed up at the time.*

An instantly noticeable aspect of Hitler's oratory was his repeatedly rolled 'r'. Although this is a distinctive feature of the Austrian/Bavarian accent, elsewhere in his diction the dictator was careful to expunge the more obvious signs of a regional dialect, in order to broaden his appeal. It has been plausibly suggested, rather, that Hitler consciously adopted this practice from German stage actors of the period, many of whom used it as a projection technique.

And therein lies the nub of Hitler's true impact as a public speaker: his mastery of the theatrical. We search in vain in his speeches for the kind of resonant, poetic turn of phrase for which Churchill became famous. Certainly, Hitler was well aware of the power of the spoken word. In *Mein Kampf*, he made it clear that he considered it far superior to writing as a propaganda tool, calling it a 'magical torch' that had 'the power to inflame' – but it was always deployed within a total performance, a Wagnerian *Gesamtkunstwerk* that went far beyond oratory. Easily as important as what was being said – possibly even more so – was the setting in which it was uttered, and the attendant panoply of stagecraft. At the Zeppelinfeld, the site of the Nuremberg party rallies (*see* Chapter 13: Rallying Point), various elements – a massive colonnaded grandstand and speaker's podium, well-choreographed ranks of storm troopers or athletes, and huge vertical swastika banners – combined to produce a spectacle in which the Führer's speech formed the grand finale. From 1936 to 1938 (the last party congress before

53

the war) the theatricality of Nuremberg quite literally reached new heights, with the entire parade ground illuminated for night rallies by 152 regularly-spaced searchlights shining vertically into the heavens to create a dazzling 'light-cathedral' (*Lichtdom*).

But smoke and mirrors can only achieve so much. Architect Albert Speer, chief stage manager of the Nuremberg rallies, ultimately found himself checkmated by his master's megalomania. The plan to redesign Berlin as the city of Germania, the capital of the Thousand-Year Reich, envisaged a north-south ceremonial axis culminating in a domed 'People's Hall' (*Volkshalle*) of gargantuan proportions (290 metres (951 feet) tall and accommodating an audience of 180,000). Aside from insurmountable civil engineering problems (no foundations, however deep, could support the weight of such a structure on Berlin's marshy substrate; plus, in cold weather the exhalations of the huge crowd would likely have generated enough water vapour for it to rain inside the dome), Speer realised that the sheer scale of the building would work against its intended psychological *raison d'être*, namely to act as a fitting space for Hitler's presentation of himself as a colossus of history bestriding the narrow world through force of arms. Instead, dwarfed by his surroundings (and with none of the 21st century's audiovisual technology to project his image onto big screens and amplify his voice effectively), the Führer would have come across as nothing but a ranting little man.

---

*Not carefully enough, though, it would seem. Bertolt Brecht's satire *The Resistible Rise of Arturo Ui* (1941), which portrays Hitler as a Chicago gangster, includes a hilarious scene in which Ui is coached by a down-at-heel old actor: 'Excellent. You're a complete natural. We just need to do something about the arms, though – they're too stiff.

Tell you what, try cupping your hands in front of your genitals (*Ui does as he's bidden*). Not bad . . . casual, yet stylish.' (This was one of Hitler's characteristic gestures; the idea was to appear statesmanlike.)

The Bully Pulpit and the Fireside Chat
[FDR's presidential style]

Three-times US President and invaluable ally of Winston Churchill, Franklin Delano Roosevelt was not the first in his family to be elected as Commander-in-Chief of the US. His distant cousin, Theodore Roosevelt, had twice occupied the Oval Office (1901–09). The earlier Roosevelt was indirectly responsible for the creation of the children's teddy bear (not such a cosy reference, since Teddy was an enthusiastic bear hunter) as well as coining the phrase 'the bully pulpit'. This particular pulpit – 'bully' is not pejorative since it's used in the sense of great (as in 'Bully for you!') – describes any position of authority that gives its occupant the dominant role when speaking out on an issue. The American Presidency is the supreme bully pulpit, and the expression is still familiar in the US.

FDR was an adroit user of the advantages which presidential status conferred on him. Confident and optimistic by nature, he led his country out of the Great Depression of the 1930s and, when war overtook Europe, steered a course between those who demanded that America keep out of the fighting and his own instinctive desire to defend democracy and combat fascism on a global, and not just a national, scale. In the end, Roosevelt's hand, and his country's, was forced by the Japanese attack on Pearl Harbor. Roosevelt initiated what became known as the 'fireside chat', a talk in which he spoke directly to the people via radio. This relatively new medium combined immediacy and intimacy, as suggested by the connotations of 'fireside chat', and guaranteed an audience greater than almost any number of political rallies put together.

Roosevelt delivered the first of these talks in March 1933, in the middle of the banking crash, and his style was clear and confiding, beginning 'My friends . . .' and reassuring his listeners that their money was safer in the bank than 'under the mattress'. From then on the number of presidential talks averaged two or three a year so when war came the radio address was the natural way of keeping the nation informed, as well as giving encouragement and invoking the patriotic spirit.

Roosevelt tended to avoid the verbal flourishes which were Churchill's stock-in-trade but he could be an inspirational leader, as evidenced by the broadcast he made following Pearl Harbor (Fireside Chat 19), with its concluding echoes of the Declaration of Independence and Lincoln's Gettysburg Address:

So we are going to win the war and we are going to win the peace that follows. And in the difficult hours of this day – through dark days that may be yet to come – we will know that the vast majority of the members of the human race are on our side. Many of them are fighting with us. All of them are praying for us. But, in representing our cause, we represent theirs as well – our hope and their hope for liberty under God.

Chapter 5

Service Slang

Military research is a famous driver of innovation and development in science, often with benefits to civilian life, realised not at the time but later. Among much else, such research is said to have produced duct tape (for fastening boxes of ammunition) and, at the opposite end of the spectrum, the first glimmerings of the Internet. Similarly, the heightened conditions of warfare provide a boost to the human propensity to use jargon, slang and bad language. In warfare, the new and unfamiliar require fresh terminology, while fear and frustration provide plenty of excuses for what Americans call 'cusswords', often surprisingly detailed and inventive.

Can We Have Our Pilot Back, Please?
[American/British: Blood chits/Goolie chits]

As the RAF quickly found during the Battle of Britain, the worst attrition in a prolonged air defence campaign wasn't on materiel, but on men. Fighter production was successfully dispersed to a number of so-called 'shadow factories' to evade Luftwaffe bombing, but Britain came perilously close to losing the battle due to the terrible toll the fighting took on invaluable experienced pilots. Many British pilot losses were wholly

57

unnecessary, with 'downed' pilots drowning in the English Channel and other bodies of water before the introduction of an effective Air–Sea Rescue Service.

But at least, fighting above home turf, RAF pilots who were shot down and reached dry land didn't have to fear assault by enraged civilians. In remote places where rural populations had no inkling of airmen's identities, perhaps even little idea that a conflict was engulfing other parts of their country, a pilot who was forced to bail out needed some way of conveying who he was in the hope of warding off attack and obtaining help. Most famously, during their expeditionary campaign against the Japanese Air Force in China in 1941–44, the men of Lieutenant-General Claire Chennault's 1st American Volunteer Group (AVG) – known as the 'Flying Tigers' from the predator's teeth and eyes insignia painted around the air intakes of their planes – wore the Chinese Nationalist flag sewn onto the back of their leather flying jackets to identify themselves as 'friendlies'. This was accompanied by a text in Chinese characters which conveyed the following message:

> *This foreign person (American) has come to China to help in the war effort. Soldiers and civilians, one and all, should rescue, protect, and provide him with medical care.*

In this same Chinese–Burmese–Indian theatre of war, British pilots carried a rayon handkerchief, printed with a similar message in a variety of local languages. The British version even dangled the promise of monetary reward in future to those who helped their airmen.

The Americans called this message a 'blood chit', adopting

in the second element an Anglo-Indian word of late 18th-century origin: chitty, or chit, meaning 'a letter or note, a certificate given to a servant or the like; a pass' (*OED*). British usage was far more colourful; supposedly dating from the RAF's operations over the wild North-West Frontier region of India and Afghanistan in World War One, where downed fliers went in fear of being castrated by fierce Pathan tribeswomen, the pass was known as a 'goolie chit'. 'Goolie' is another Indian loanword, denoting the testicles: once widely used in British English, and redolent of 'Steptoe and Son', it has sadly fallen into disuse.

Odd Bods
[British/American: Chad and Kilroy]

A bizarre example of the US-British alliance acting in unofficial concert is provided by the merging of two wartime imaginary figures, Kilroy and Mr Chad, from America and Britain respectively. Mr Chad was a cartoon figure, reduced to a head and a large U-shaped nose and clutching fingers, peering over a fence or wall. The caption above his head or scribbled on the wall beneath read 'WOT! NO . . .' followed by BEER or CIGGIES or PETROL or whatever item was in short supply – in wartime, for instance, almost everything. Occasionally his bald head was surmounted by a single hair curled in the shape of a question mark.

As usual with such legendary creations, there is no agreement about the origin of Mr Chad. One theory holds that he was the creation of a cartoonist called George Chatterton and known as 'Chat', a nickname which could transform into Chad easily enough. A more elaborate idea has the image growing out of the electrical symbol for AC current and voltage (a series of curves cut across by a straight line), which would suggest that Chad was the brainchild of a bored technical trainee, possibly one in the RAF. As for the name, that might come from an instructor called Chadwick or from Chadwick House, part of a radio school in Lancashire, or perhaps from someone or somewhere else . . .

An article in *Life* magazine (March 1946), commenting on the conflicting 'folklore' surrounding the name, pointed out that 'Chad is no officer's pet'. This was one reason for his ubiquity and popularity. He represented protest in a mild but unmistakably cynical form. The same article tells of the commanding officer of an army camp who gives his men a dressing-down at a special parade. 'This Chad business has gone too far. From now on, anyone pinning up these silly things will get 28 days C.B. [confined to barracks].' Returning to his office, the CO finds on his blotting paper the lugubrious face and impudent question 'Wot, only 28 days?'

The American Kilroy was a quite different creation, at least in the beginning. He shared Chad's popularity and ubiquity, and the pair would eventually achieve union, when the Chad face peering over the wall would be complemented with the boast KILROY WAS HERE. But Kilroy started as a piece of graffiti, one that did no more than assert his presence. As with Mr Chad, there are various explanations for his existence.* The least implausible traces him to an inspector, James J. Kilroy, in a Massachusetts shipyard who scrawled 'Kilroy was here' in yellow chalk on the work which he had checked. But even this explanation doesn't hold (much) water. An inspector would be more likely to put his initials, JJK, or simply scribble OK on what he'd seen. In all probability, Kilroy did not exist. He was a mythological figure. Indeed, in 1947 Hollywood released a black-and-white comedy entitled *Kilroy Was Here* with the tagline: 'Is He Man or Myth?'

This elusiveness was integral to his appeal. Wherever you looked for him, you would not be able to find him, for the simple reason that he had already been – and gone. The graffito never read KILROY *IS* HERE. His name often appeared in places that were not easily accessible or even dangerous, like ships' interiors or enemy pillboxes. Popping up everywhere, Kilroy was confidently impudent, the stuff of legend. Reportedly, his appearance on captured American equipment caused Hitler to think that he was a particularly successful Allied spy. Stalin is also supposed to have spotted Kilroy in the VIP lavatory at the Potsdam conference and made enquiries about him. It would be nice if at least one of these stories was true.

But the British Mr Chad, drawing attention to universal shortages, tended more towards wry insubordination. You could see this as emblematic of the differences between the emerging superpower on one side of the Atlantic and the declining imperial power on the other side. Nevertheless, the figures of Chad and Kilroy did form a successful alliance and the large-nosed cartoon character accompanied by the legend KILROY WAS HERE can now be seen on two tucked-away places on the World War Two memorial in Washington.

According to the lexicographer and slang expert Eric Partridge, there were other names for Mr Chad's peering head: Private Snoops (for the army) and The Watcher (for the navy). And in Australia was to be found the slogan FOO WAS HERE, the name possibly deriving from a 1930s cartoon strip. But

none of them has the staying power of Kilroy. He is still here
– or rather, he was here.

*Similarly with Uncle Sam, another representative and ubiquitous
figure, although, in this case, of governmental authority. Samuel
Wilson was a supplier of meat to the American army during the early
19th century, and the 'US' initials, standing for United States and
stamped on the barrels of meat, were conflated with a jokey reference
to the 'Uncle Sam' who was feeding the troops – or so the story goes.

Steam Chickens and Flying Coffins
[British/American/German: Aircraft nicknames]

In the old days, as those of us who avidly read *Biggles* books
in our youth know, pilots were a breed apart: roustabout,
happy-go-lucky fellows who scoffed in the face of danger –
the only way to be when you were required to go aloft in
dreadful conditions and wrestle with the controls of machines
that were extremely primitive by modern standards. And
often get shot at into the bargain. (How different in the fly-by-
wire cockpit environment of today, where avionics does much
of the thinking for the pilot, sometimes with disastrous
consequences.)

An intrinsic part of the World War Two pilot's demeanour
was his (or her – women served with great distinction in the
only service where they were permitted to fly, the Air Transport
Auxiliary (ATA), delivering warplanes to airfields) rich fund of
slang and irreverent sense of humour, often of the gallows
variety. The cockpit was the 'office' and the plane, however
streamlined or swift, the 'crate'. Similarly, the best efforts of
aircraft designers to come up with inventive solutions to air

ministries' often unrealistic specifications frequently met with mockery by those destined to fly them – in the form of unflattering nicknames. Here, then, is a selection of some of the more insulting and outlandish of these aeronautical *noms de guerre*.

- **Stringbag** (British: Fairey Swordfish) The Swordfish was one of several aging aircraft types that Britain's air forces – in this case, the Fleet Air Arm of the Royal Navy – found themselves still operating when war broke out. A torpedo bomber and reconnaissance aircraft, this lumbering single-engined biplane belonged to another era, with its slow speed (good for landing on carriers, not so good for evading trouble) and its struts and wires. The nickname, though, wasn't an allusion to its old-fashioned construction, but to the large amount of equipment and ordnance this robust workhorse could carry, like a housewife's string-net shopping bag. For all its obsolescence, though, and as testament to the bravery of the aircrew, in November 1940 just 24 of these planes managed to deal a crippling blow against the Italian battle fleet anchored at its base at Taranto.

- **Flying Pencil** (German: Dornier Do17) The Versailles Treaties of 1919 banned Germany from manufacturing military aircraft. After Hitler came to power, and before he repudiated all the terms of the post-World War One settlement, clandestine development of bombers, fighters and other warplanes proceeded under the guise of civil types. Claude Dornier's slimline Do17 was ostensibly designed as a fast mail plane for Lufthansa. In the event, the airline rejected it because the passenger cabin, which was meant to accommodate six people, was impossibly narrow and cramped. Its long, slender fuselage was built for speed, effectively reducing drag. Repurposed as a bomber, as was always intended, the Do17's distinctive shape soon earned it the name *Fliegender Bleistift* ('Flying Pencil'). This form of soubriquet was common in aviation circles: the World War Two British medium bomber, the Handley Page Hampden, was called the 'Flying Suitcase' because of its deep, narrow main fuselage, while the wooden construction and slab sides of the Airspeed Horsa troop-carrying glider – quite apart from its worrisome lack of an engine – led to it being dubbed the 'Flying Coffin'.

- **Jug** (American: Republic P-47 Thunderbolt) Here's a nickname that was truly tailor-made for the aircraft in question. This muscular, barrel-chested plane, equipped with a meaty power plant, was the largest and heaviest single piston-engined fighter ever built. Fitted with fuel drop-tanks, it provided escort fighter cover for bombers of the US Eighth Air Force as they flew from their East Anglian bases on daylight raids deep into Germany, such as the attacks on the vital ball-bearing factory at Schweinfurt in 1943. It was a well-liked aircraft, and its nickname may be derived from the popular tune 'Little Brown Jug', recorded by the American big-band leader Glenn Miller in 1939 ('*Ha, ha, ha, hee, hee, hee/Little Brown Jug, don't I love thee?*'; possibly an additional reference here to the olive-drab colour scheme of USAAF planes that arrived in Britain). Some people, understandably but wrongly, thought that it was short for 'juggernaut'. An easy mistake to make: it was reputed that, once you pushed the control stick forward in a Jug, nothing could out-dive you.

- **Shagbat** (British: Supermarine Walrus) Before he went on to create the supremely beautiful Spitfire, Supermarine designer R.J. Mitchell produced a series of flying boats for the same Southampton-based firm. Flying boats weren't exactly the most elegant things in the skies: the clue's in the actual term – boats aren't meant to fly, and the result is usually a lash-up of the worst features of an aeroplane and a waterborne craft. But the Walrus was a minger even in the company of these other ugly ducklings. So much so that its crews devised a portmanteau word that combined an ungainly-looking seabird with a hideous-faced nocturnal flying mammal, as its nickname. Its other, less common names, the 'Steam Pigeon' and Steam Chicken', referred to the vapour produced by sea spray hitting its large, hot radial engine. Still, however unprepossessing its looks, downed RAF pilots facing a watery grave were delighted to see the Shagbat when it performed air–sea rescue duties in the Channel.

- **Meatbox** (British: Gloster Meteor) The twin-engined Meteor was the Allies' first operational jet, entering service in mid-1944. It was deployed both at home, to counter the threat from fast, unmanned V-1 flying bombs ('Doodlebugs'), and in the invasion of Germany, to oppose the Germans' own jet fighter, the Messerschmitt Me262 – though there is no record of them ever meeting in combat. 'Meatbox' was originally probably just a jokey corruption of the aircraft's real name, but took on a decidedly sinister new dimension when, in the late 1940s and early 1950s, it claimed the lives of a large number of novice pilots, due to its high instability at low speeds, say when landing, with one engine throttled back ('asymmetric flight').

- **Stuka** (German: Junkers Ju87) Not a nickname, strictly speaking, but a contraction of the kind of compound noun that gives the German language a bad name. (A classic example was the Nazi Air Ministry, the *Reichsluftfahrt-ministerium*; no wonder Germans love an acronym.) The *Sturzkampfflugzeug*, literally 'dive bombing aircraft', was designed with that sole purpose in mind. The unmistakable Stuka, with its inverted gull wings, fixed spatted undercarriage and long, glass canopy housing two crew (a pilot and a rear gunner) first flew in 1935. During the invasion of Poland in 1939 and the *Blitzkrieg* of 1940 against the Low Countries it gained a fearsome reputation as a terroriser of civilian populations. To add to the fear factor, wind-driven wailing sirens known as 'Jericho trumpets' (*Jericho-Trompeten*) were fitted to the planes. But when, as in the Battle of Britain, the Ju87 came up against effective fighter opposition, it was a sitting duck. Diverting the Stuka to a more conventional ground-attack role and beefing up its firepower to deal with armour, the Germans called a later variant of the aircraft the *Panzerknacker* ('tank-buster') or the *Kanonenvogel* ('cannon-bird').

Throughout the war, the British weekly magazine *Aeroplane* contained a popular feature – 'Oddentification' – by their in-house cartoonist E.A. Wren (1909–82). Intended as an identification aid to spotters and gunners in anti-aircraft batteries, Wren's column included a caricature of an aircraft and an accompanying rhyme, pointing out some of its prominent features. For instance, the Stuka entry runs:

A crooked wing, a square-cut tail,
Fat legs below and a bomb to trail,
Deep-jowled before a glasshouse hump,
The Stuka's an ungainly lump.

Whispering Campaign
[American/Australian/British:
Scuttlebutt/Furphy/Elsan gen/Sibs]

Rumour must be as old as warfare. Wherever you have ordinary soldiers gathered together, waiting to be sent somewhere or already on the march, or the eve of battle, they will inevitably speculate about what they're going to do and what is going to happen to them. In the absence of hard information, which they are not likely to get, they will circulate all sorts of wild stories. Several slightly bizarre expressions to do with gossip and rumour sprang up in the early 20th century and were current during World War Two. One which long ago entered the American linguistic mainstream is 'scuttlebutt', once a piece of nautical slang and now increasingly found in British English. A scuttled – or holed – butt is the seagoing term for a cask from which water can be drawn. The cask was later replaced by a drinking fountain but the original expression survived. Since sailors naturally stopped and chatted while they drew water, their gossip and rumourmongering took its nickname from the spot where they were standing.

Another water-based term for rumour is 'furphy', still current in Australia. John Furphy was a manufacturer of mobile water tanks which were originally created for transporting water on farms before being employed on a large scale by the Australian army in World War One, particularly in the

Gallipoli campaign. Once they'd been towed into camp the water carts were usually parked close to the latrines, perhaps the one area where the men could gossip away from the watchful eye of the officers. In addition, the drivers of the 'furphies' were themselves notorious for spreading rumours wherever they went.

There are a couple of peculiar sanitary equivalents to 'furphy', also drawn from service slang. 'Elsan gen' refers to information that cannot be relied on and derives from the trade name of the portable lavatories that use chemicals to neutralise the waste. Elsans (an amalgamation of the first two initials of the inventor Ephraim Louis Jackson and sanitation) were being installed on bombers at around the same time as 'gen' emerged as RAF slang for 'information'. So the flying lavatory became the rumour centre. A 1943 guide to service slang defines it as 'news invented in the gentlemen's toilet'. Another term from World War Two is 'latrinogram', a technically advanced version of the 'latrine rumour' which first saw the light of day in 1918.* The common denominator for these expressions is that the news they purvey is likely to be wide of the mark or just plain wrong.

A wartime rumour which was started deliberately in the hope that it would get back to the enemy and mislead him was known in the intelligence trade as a 'sib', short for 'sibilant' and named for the whispered, hissing sound of information passed over in secret. These 'sibs' weren't casually thrown off, but created by intelligence/propaganda departments, often with physical evidence to back them up. For example, as a deterrent to a German invasion in 1940, the rumour was started that the British possessed a weapon that could set the English Channel on fire. Indeed, there had been experiments with flame-throwers and tanks of oil, experiments which did not work – i.e. it proved impossible to set the sea alight – but they were conducted in places on the south coast where they could be observed from a distance. At the same time, the RAF incendiary bombing of German shipping in harbours on the north coast of France caused burns to troops which, when they were being treated in Paris hospitals, resulted in a story being spread that the injuries had occurred during a disastrous invasion attempt. It must have helped that a few burned bodies (of shot-down Luftwaffe pilots) were actually washed ashore in Britain, and that the few quickly became many in the stories which reached German ears. This was an example of a carefully thought-out sib. By contrast, the story about the Channel being full of man-eating sharks transported from Australia was an example from the crackpot corner of the sib-factory.

*German soldiers in World War Two had a similar expression for unsubstantiated rumours: *eine Latrinenparole,* literally 'latrine password'.

Swearing Like Troopers
[American/British: C**t cap/Shit on a shingle/ Effing and blinding]

It is certain – and almost certainly unprovable – that bad language flourished in the war in a way that it had never done during years of uneasy peace. The frustrations of wartime life and service, the forced association of large groups of (mostly) young males, the relaxing of some older standards of speech, all contributed to unprecedented levels of what the British call 'effing and blinding' or the frequent use of 'fuck', in all its variant forms, and 'blimey'.

During the war the British displayed a particular expertise and ease in swearing, especially among the Other Ranks (i.e. the non-officers). This was recognised by the authorities. After a German spy had managed to deceive a British unit during the North African campaign because he spoke impeccable Other Ranks English, a pamphlet from the War Office issued a warning: 'It should [. . .] be impressed on all ranks that the use in conversation of "f-----s" and "b------s" is *not* necessarily a guarantee of British nationality.'

The Americans went one step further and tried to ban bad language altogether. The 1944 edition of *The Bluejacket's Manual*, a handbook for navy personnel, stated flatly: 'The use of profane or filthy language is forbidden.' Despite this, language and obscenity went on in their normal way, hand in hand. As Paul Fussell* observes in *Wartime* (1989), a 'demeaning impulse, a compound of both hatred and fear' produced language appropriate to the services:

> *The soldier's overseas cap, the one that opens up along the top, is called a cunt cap; it's hard to imagine any other piece of conventional headgear, like a policeman's visor cap or a bishop's miter or a motorcyclist's helmet treated automatically with such obscene disrespect.*

The written word was a different matter. Censorship and decorum prevented the printing of obscene words in both America and Britain, except sometimes in small-edition publications intended for a select audience. When Norman Mailer wrote *The Naked and the Dead* (1948), his classic novel about the war in the Pacific, he used the euphemism 'fug'. A well-known story has the first-time author approached by the actress Tallulah Bankhead with the words: 'Oh, hello, you're Norman Mailer. You're the young man that doesn't know how to spell fuck.' By the early 1960s things had changed, and Joseph Heller's *Catch 22* (1961) was the first major war novel to capitalise on the freedom to write in the way that people actually spoke.

Other terms, though considered coarse, were nevertheless allowable. In British English, 'bugger' has never carried much of a charge and, depending on context, can sound almost affectionate (as in 'silly old bugger'). The verb form was a favourite of Churchill's; he would sometimes end phone calls with the initials KBO, or 'Keep Buggering On'. By contrast, the ubiquitous American use of 'shit' has always tended to be more dismissive, and two such coinages from the war era are 'chickenshit', to denote someone or something inadequate or cowardly, and the expressive 'shit on a shingle' for minced beef on toast. Meanwhile, payday for soldiers was 'the day the eagle shits'.

*Paul Fussell (1924–2012) was an American academic who wrote about the war from bitter experience. His fine memoir, *Doing Battle* (1996), describes his time as a GI in Europe and the lifelong effect of the conflict on him. *The Great War and Modern Memory* (1975) shows how much of modern culture and thinking was shaped by World War One, while studies such as *Wartime* and *The Boys' Crusade* (2003) examine the fighting not from the perspective of the commander's bunker but through the eyes of the average 'grunt', as they would be called in later wars.

Chapter 6

National Stereotypes

The all too human tendency to slag people off because they are 'they' and different from 'us' receives an immeasurable boost in wartime. Being abusive about the enemy becomes a patriotic duty as well as a necessary pleasure. Even to be rude about one's allies is both an assertion of national pride and also a way of relieving the strains and tension inherent in any shared effort.

'A Horrible Sight'

[German: *der Stechschritt*, 'Goose-stepping']

For us Anglo-Saxons, goose-stepping up and down will forever be associated with Nazism. The bombastic, triumphalist, inhumanly mechanistic nature of this military drill sums up everything we hated about fascists. So powerful is the image that it, along with 'the jackboot', still serves as a trope for this dark period of German history. Notoriously, in the last programme of the first series of *Fawlty Towers* ('The Germans'; 1975) John Cleese as hotel owner Basil Fawlty reprised the preternaturally gangly gait he had first used in the *Monty Python* 'Ministry of Silly Walks' sketch by goose-stepping and down the dining room in xenophobic fury at some German guests' perfectly reasonable and polite request. The effect was hilariously offensive; German television could only bring itself to air this episode for the first time in 1993, and even then it was left to a cable channel to screen it.

But let's dispel some myths straight away. First, the goose-step is by no means exclusively German. Fifty or so armies around the world still use it – chiefly, it must be said, in banana republics, military dictatorships or some other stripe of totalitarian state; unsurprisingly, the German Federal army (*Bundeswehr*) is not one of them. Second, it wasn't invented by the Nazis: the prolific Victorian author and hymn lyricist, the Reverend Sabine Baring-Gould (who, appropriately enough, wrote 'Onward, Christian Soldiers') mentions seeing Prussian 'recruits ... goose-stepping, posturing' in his 1879 book *Germany*.

The English term is an odd one: a goose's gait is more of a comical waddle than a purposeful stride. The ancient Romans may well have kept geese on the Capitoline Hill to warn against attack, but their ferocity doesn't extend beyond kicking up an almighty flapping fuss of hissing and pecking. In fact, all the term alludes to is the goose's habit of alternately putting all its weight on one leg and lifting the other completely off the ground when walking. German has a completely different word for the goose-step, *der Stechschritt*, literally meaning 'stab-step.' (A *faux ami* for the unwary translator also lurks in the German phrase '*im Gänsemarsch*' – literally 'in the manner of geese marching' – which actually refers to bodies in formation, be it people, ships or aircraft, and best translates as 'in single file' or 'line astern'.)

George Orwell's five-year stint in the Indian Imperial Police in Burma imbued him with a lifelong revulsion of all forms of militarism. In his 1946 essay 'Why I Write', he noted that the goose-step could only exist in countries whose people were too frightened to laugh at the antics of their soldiery. Five years earlier, in 'The Lion and the Unicorn,' he put it even more plainly. 'The goose-step,' he wrote, 'is one of the most horrible sights in the world.'

Name-Calling

[American/British: Nazi/Eyetie/Wop/Nip, etc.]

Of the three principal enemy nations faced by the Allies in World War Two, it was the Germans who seemed to provoke the most ambiguous response among the British and the Americans. The derogatory nicknames for them, such as Fritz, Hun, Kraut and Boche, had all surfaced before World War One. The only one which persisted into World War Two was Jerry, which though hardly affectionate is a familiar term rather than an abusive or racially charged one (dictionaries usually classify the word as slang or colloquial). Possibly no more than a diminutive form of German, especially if spelled Gerry, the word is far from being an unattractive and guttural monosyllable like Fritz or Kraut.

Arguably the most hostile expression was Nazi, a shortened form of Hitler's *Nationalsozialistische Deutsche Arbeiterpartei*; it first appeared as early as 1930 in *The Times*. All of its associated terms (Nazism, Nazidom, Nazification) emerged soon afterwards and, when they occurred in English, the context tended to be negative long before the outbreak of war in 1939. The term was not used by the Nazis about themselves, but initially by their German opponents and this usage may have been shaped by a Bavarian diminutive of the name Ignatius; this little 'Nazi' denotes a clumsy individual.

Although overlapping in meaning with 'fascist', Nazi carried – and continues to carry – a stronger charge, particularly when spoken aloud. Winston Churchill uttered the word with distinctive animosity as '*Narzee*'. Such mild mispronunciation as a way of disparaging the enemy had its counterpart in World War One, with the Prime Minister, Lloyd George, always referring to the Kaiser as the '*Kayser*'. It was by misusing the secret-police term Gestapo, a term even more fearsome than Nazi, that Churchill made a rare blunder in public speaking. In his first party-political broadcast during the election campaign of June 1945, the wartime leader claimed that the introduction of socialism into Britain – via the election of a Labour government under Clement Attlee – would require some form of Gestapo, 'no doubt very humanely directed in the first instance'. This was such a descent from 'We shall fight on the beaches' oratory to naked scaremongering that it caused 'disappointment and real distress' among listeners, according to polls. There is little doubt that the Gestapo made its own very minor contribution to Churchill's ousting from No. 10 in the July of 1945.

Whatever the poisonous associations of Nazi, Gestapo or SS (*Schutzstaffel* or 'defence squad'), there were also abstract qualities for which the Germans were known and often admired, qualities like efficiency and discipline. Though easily translatable for the purposes of wartime propaganda into coldness and a robot-like willingness to follow orders, these attributes still commanded a respect which was justified by the string of successes achieved by German forces in the first half of the war.

With the Italians things were different. There were fewer slang terms for them, with the reductive 'Eyetie' (i.e. I-talian) being used by the British, Australians and Americans, and 'wop' more of a US speciality (possibly deriving from an Italian dialect term, *guappo*, meaning bold and showy). An older term 'macaroni' was sometimes used, with an obvious pasta reference. Fairly or not, the Italians were regarded as a different class of enemy to the Germans, even if at the beginning of the war several of the senior staff in London's most prestigious hotels had been interned because of their Italian origins. By contrast, President Roosevelt decided not to intern US Italian resident aliens in 1942, characterising them as 'a lot of opera singers'. Representative of general attitudes towards this key Axis member was the name for a new dance craze sweeping London following the Italian retreat in Libya. According to an article in the *Sydney Morning Herald* in February 1941, it was known as the 'Tuscana' and involved a couple of steps back for every step forward, and the accompanying words: 'That's just the cutest dance, because you don't advance – You just retreat.'

There was the feeling that Italy was cut out for finer, more enjoyable pursuits than waging war. When the bombardier Joseph Heller, author of the famous anti-war satire *Catch 22*, arrived in Rome after its liberation in 1944 he found that their executive officer had rented comfortable apartments for the squadron, complete with cooks and maids. Their appetite had already been whetted by stories of men returning from rest leave in the eternal city and 'speaking, rhapsodically and disbelievingly, of restaurants, nightclubs, dance halls, and girls, girls, girls – girls in their summer dresses strolling with smiles on the Via Veneto' (*Now and Then, A Memoir*, 1998).

With the Japanese it was different yet again. Views of the Germans or the Italians as the enemy were governed not only by what they did, or were reported have done in news and propaganda, but by national stereotyping. More potently, when it came to the war in the Pacific, racial hostility was added to nationalism. The Japanese were beyond being mere foreigners, they were almost a different species. The cartoon cover of *Collier's* magazine for 12 December 1942, commemorating the first anniversary of Pearl Harbor, shows Tojo, the Japanese Prime Minister, as a fanged vampire bat clutching a bomb which he is about to release on the unsuspecting US fleet. References to 'monkey-men' or 'subhumans' recall the German classification of *Untermenschen* for those they regarded as racially inferior. While Tojo's name was used, particularly by Australians, to mean a Japanese soldier or airman, 'Jap' was the standard disparaging expression among the Allies, useful for punchy slogans like 'Let's Blast the Jap Clean Off the Map'. 'Nip' was common too and derived from Nippon, a shortened form of *Nippon-koku* ('land of the origin of the sun').

When it came to the Allies, the slang terms were already familiar: Aussie for Australian, Kiwi for New Zealand (after the bird which is the national emblem), Canuck for Canadian, and Russky/i or sometimes Ivan (= John) for the Russians. These long predated World War Two, as do Yank and Tommy. The first is a colloquialism for any American (civilian or military) but Tommy specifies a soldier and derives from 'Thomas Atkins', the name used in the army from the early 19th century as an example in specimen forms.

Adolf Hitler, Rah, Rah, Rah!

[**German:** *der Hitlergruß/Sieg Heil!*,
the 'Hitler greeting'; the Nazi salute and greeting]

There is every reason to suppose that the Nazis got the idea for their straight-armed, right-handed salute (*der Hitlergruß*; 'Hitler greeting') and the attendant cry of *Sieg Heil!* (literally 'Hail Victory!') from similar practices among the fascists of Italy. There, the so-called Roman salute (*saluto romano*) was adopted by Mussolini's regime as the required way of honouring the flag, in schools and elsewhere, from 1923 onwards. Inevitably, it derived from a gesture first used by the writer Gabriele d'Annunzio during his occupation of Fiume in 1919 (where, incidentally, he also styled himself '*Duce*'). D'Annunzio himself appropriated the salute from the early Italian cinematic epic of ancient Rome *Cabiria* (1914), for which he himself wrote the screenplay; there is no historical evidence to indicate that either Republican or Imperial Romans ever greeted one another in this way. In Germany, the first recorded use of 'Sieg Heil!' was by Joseph Goebbels at an NSDAP rally in the run-up to the parliamentary elections of 1932.

A far more offbeat provenance was suggested by the German–American businessman and Harvard alumnus Ernst Franz Sedgwick Hanfstaengl (1887–1975). An early acolyte and confidant of Hitler (who knew the former by his affectionate nickname of 'Putzi'), Hanfstaengl later fell from favour and defected in 1937. After internment in Britain, he was granted asylum in 1942 by the United States and debriefed by the Office for Strategic Services (OSS), a forerunner of the CIA. During this interview, he made the extraordinary claim that

'Sieg Heil!' had been his creation, and was based on the football chants he had heard and admired in his youth:

I had Hitler fairly shouting with enthusiasm: 'That's it, Hanfstaengl, that's what we need for the movement, marvellous' and he pranced up and down the room like a drum majorette. The 'Rah, rah, rah!' refrain of Harvardmen became the thunderous 'Sieg Heil! Sieg Heil!' of the Brownshirt demonstrations.

Hanfstaengl's implicit likening of American football hearties to Nazi storm troopers may well have been a belated and none-too-subtle act of revenge against his *alma mater*, which in 1934 had turned down a donation of $1,000 from him out of revulsion for his politics. Still, anyone who has witnessed Ivy League jocks – or, for that matter, Oxbridge rugger-buggers – in full cry will appreciate the verisimilitude of his comparison.

Chapter 7

Food and Drink

A generation of postwar British children, including the current authors, endured mealtimes with the exhortations of our parents ringing in our ears, insisting that we eat up every scrap of food on our plates – soggy, over-boiled greens, lumpy mashed potato and all. At the time, it seemed nothing short of blackmail, a hurdle we had to leap in order to get access to the tooth-rotting treats we really craved: Bird's Instant Whip, Rowntree's Jelly or Wall's Neapolitan ice cream. But, of course, such abhorrence of waste was only natural to people who had lived through a period when merchant ships daily ran the gauntlet of U-boats in the Atlantic to bring vital war supplies, and food imports or large-scale domestic meat production were out of the question. Still, it's heartening to find that people back then moaned about the poor fare on offer, too.

'Food Will Win the War'

[American/British: Woolton Pie/snoek/
British Restaurants]

The received picture of wartime eating and drinking in Britain is one of shortages, rationing and make-do ingenuity (e.g. nettle toast, dandelion fritters). But the paradoxical truth is that a large number of people were better fed and more healthy during the war than they had ever been in peacetime. The principal reason was the growing role taken by the government in subsidising the cost of vital foods and ensuring more equitable distribution ('Fair Shares for All'), as well as funding advertising campaigns which successfully encouraged healthy eating while discouraging waste.

As early as 1917, with the entry of the United States into World War One, the American government had recognised the importance of controlling nutrition, if only to ensure that resources were redirected away from consumption and towards the war effort. 'Food Will Win the War' was a typical slogan aimed at making people eat less, reinforced by specific appeals for the 'Meatless Monday' or 'Wheatless Wednesday'. On the other side of the Atlantic, war or no war, such privations were less likely to be voluntary. During the 1930s, the social conscience of some in Britain was pricked by research showing that as much as half the population was badly fed, and up to 10 percent severely undernourished, even if the government rejected such statistics.

World War Two changed things for the better. This wasn't entirely a matter of public welfare and benign government. The authorities saw that an unhealthy, undernourished population would soon become a demoralised one, and thus poorly equipped for the fight or even the day-to-day slog of existence. In addition, while the disparity between the well-off and those who often struggled to afford the basics, let alone luxuries, might be tolerated in peacetime, it could not be justified during a conflict in which the authorities were demanding equal effort and sacrifice from all. Paradoxically, rationing and shortages also helped public health since the things which were in regular supply, like vegetables and wholemeal bread, were better for consumers than the meat or sugar or butter which were doled out in smaller and smaller portions as the war continued.

Rationing was imposed in a piecemeal way from 1940, beginning with bacon, ham, butter and sugar, although some goods, mainly those which were tinned or dried, remained unregulated until the end of 1941. Bread went unrationed during the war though, ironically, was subject to rationing after it. Other foods such as fish or chicken were not officially controlled but in practice there was no reliable supply. For example, wartime conditions meant the shrinkage both of the fishing fleets, because of labour demands, and of the areas where it was safe to fish. The only thing which shortages could be guaranteed to produce in abundance were queues. In the words of Robert Mackay, author of *Half the Battle* (2002), a study of civilian morale:

> *Queuing for food was one of the home front's characteristic activities, if standing still for hours can be so described. It followed not just from the fluctuations in the supply of certain foods but from the fact that retailers, wanting to appear fair, did not allow customers to build up stocks by buying a large amount at a time.*

More exotic foods were simply unobtainable or very rarely seen in the shops. Imported produce like lemons and bananas or coffee and cocoa were not subject to rationing because they were not available in sufficient quantity to justify it. Consequently, when these items did appear they carried a whiff of luxury. In his autobiography *Will This Do?*, Auberon Waugh remembered when, just after the end of the war, his mother managed to get hold of three bananas, one for each of her children. This precious fruit, never before seen or tasted by the children, was instead piled onto the plate of Auberon's father, Evelyn Waugh. Under the distraught gaze of Auberon and the others, the great satirical novelist proceeded to cover the plate with sugar and cream (also strictly rationed) and finished off the lot.

Wartime is a great spur to innovation in most areas, even if some of the food creations have a desperate air to them. Mutton was smoked and salted liked bacon, and the result called macon. It did not catch on except in a small way in Scotland, from where the recipe for curing mutton in peat smoke was said to have originated two hundred years earlier. The variants on macon were no more satisfactory: vencon (venison bacon) and becon (beef bacon). The Minister of Food, Lord Woolton, who was responsible for rationing and for persuading the public into better eating habits, gave his name to the Woolton Pie, the ingredients of which 'could be varied according to the vegetables in season' (i.e. anything going apart from meat). Attempts were made to fill the gap left by the shortage of more palatable fish with whale meat and snoek, a barracuda-like fish tinned and imported from South Africa. Snoek (pronounced and sometimes spelled 'snook') never caught on, despite the best efforts of the authorities, and the proper market for this leathery and ancient-tasting delicacy – domestic cats – was discovered only after the war.

The popularity of these substitutes can be judged from the way that people ditched them at the first opportunity once the war was over or when rationing finished. But, ironically, one wartime initiative has recently become a mark not of privation but affluence. In 1940, a London-based Frenchman called

Georges de Mauduit de Kervern wrote a book entitled *They Can't Ration These*. In its pages were to be found recipes for samphire soup and roasted pine kernels, hedgehog stew and roast sparrows. The Vicomte de Mauduit, one of whose earlier books was *Reminiscences of a Wandering Nobleman*, was an early proponent of foraging or getting something for nothing. Thoughtfully, the Vicomte also included various herbal remedies and tisane preparations to counter the stresses of wartime. *They Can't Ration These* originally appeared with a preface by the former Prime Minister David Lloyd George, who claimed that the foraging idea was so good that he might well have thought of it himself. The book was republished in 2004, all but half a century after the end of World War Two, and was described as the 'perfect present for the ecologically-minded'.

Shortages and rationing brought out an innate British barminess. One *Times* reader recalled that during World War One the Ministry of Food had suggested that people eat bread and butter with the butter-side down, because in this way the butter came into direct contact with the tongue and so a smaller quantity would be needed to satisfy the taste buds. Another correspondent, J.R.B. Bransom, was a zealot for grass as a regular part of the diet, either fresh off the ground or in the form of hay: 'The sample I am eating at the moment comes off a golf green at Mitcham Common. I have never suffered from urticaria [nettle rash].' This was not a joke. J.R.B. Bransom had long tried to spread the gospel of grass and had already been rebuked for it by the Minister for Health, who pointed out that the human stomach wasn't equipped to digest this particular natural product.

Yet, whatever the ingenuity or absurdity of some of the measures designed to make food shortages more tolerable, there is no doubt that people in general benefited from the government's policies. Subsidies meant that poorer people were spending less, proportionately, on their food than before the war. The Welfare Foods Scheme, which started in December 1941, ensured that pregnant women, children, invalids and others received cheap or free supplies of cod-liver oil, milk and orange juice. Even the widely disliked National Wheatmeal Loaf, a grey and rather indigestible bread made of the whole wheat grain, including the husk, was nutritionally much better than the white bread that people had previously consumed.

The Minister of Food, Lord Woolton, was a popular figure and surveys showed that most people felt that things were better than they expected. A well-run system of rationing rein-forced wartime solidarity and was even seen by some as furthering a social programme of growing equality and redis-tribution. Woolton was also shrewd enough to provide a little extra. He instituted a nationwide chain of restaurants where people could eat cheaply but without using up their precious allowance of ration points. More like communal kitchens or canteens than conventional restaurants, they were first known by the utilitarian description of 'Communal Feeding Centres'. Winston Churchill, disliking the socialist overtones of the title, suggested they should be referred to as 'British Restaurants'.

Boozing for Britain

[British: the 'Berkeley Stinger']

The British authorities adopted a tolerant attitude towards drinking during the war years. As with tobacco, they realised its value in relieving stress and providing some comfort and uplift. Almost as important was the contribution made to the exchequer by the tax on alcohol and tobacco. Consuming was a duty in both senses. Rough calculations showed that the war could be paid for if every adult smoked two packets of cigarettes and drank half a bottle of whisky daily. More specifically, an editorial in the *Brewers' Journal* pointed out that the duty on beer provided the government with slightly more than a quarter of a million pounds every day. Since the daily cost of the war was estimated at £6,000,000, no one could deny that beer drinkers were doing their bit. And not just beer. Until the fall of France in 1940 wine importers proclaimed it a patriotic duty to drink wine and champagne from Britain's principal European ally.

When it came to alcohol, the British government led by example and started at the top. Winston Churchill was famous for his capacity. His first conference with Stalin in Moscow in 1942 was sealed with endless toasts. According to Max Hastings in *Finest Years* (2009): 'Even the Soviets were impressed by the quantities of alcohol consumed both by their own leader and Churchill. One guest, unfamiliar with the Prime Minister's usual diction, wrote afterwards: 'His speech was slurred as though his mouth was full of porridge.'

The war years produced their own alcoholic and verbal innovations, of which two may serve as instances from opposite ends of the spectrum. When the survivor of a bomb blast asked the barman at London's Berkeley Hotel for something with a therapeutic sting, he was presented with a combination of brandy and crème de menthe that subsequently became known as the Berkeley Stinger. A drink to avoid, by contrast, would have been the US Navy preparation known as 'torpedo juice' and concocted – illicitly – from the ethyl alcohol employed in torpedo motors.

'Don't Mind the Worms'

[British/American: 'Dig for Victory'/Victory gardens]

During World War Two the British were officially encouraged to grow their own vegetables not only because of food shortages and because homegrown produce meant that stretched resources (labour, transport) could be diverted to the war effort, but because of the morale-boosting and health-giving benefits of 'digging for victory'. A typical poster depicted a basket full of onions, carrots, cauliflower and the like with the legend: 'Your own vegetables all the year round . . . if you DIG FOR VICTORY NOW.' The most familiar poster showed a booted foot pushing a shovel into the soil, and in this context it is pleasing to note that the 'Dig for Victory' slogan was thought up by Michael Foot (1913–2010), then a writer on the *Evening Standard* and later to become leader of the Labour Party during the early 1980s.

If you didn't have a garden you were urged to get an allotment. By 1943 there were 1,750,000 allotments, an area equivalent in size to the county of Rutland. Parks and wasteland were turned over to allotments and the moat round the Tower of London was surrendered to the vegetable growers. The tennis courts at Wimbledon were spared only after a public outcry. Though there is some doubt about the effectiveness of the grow-your-own campaign, the authorities were ingenious in their propagandising. The undergraduates of one of Oxford University's women's colleges were prompted to dig by being fed on rice as a main course, followed by rice pudding, to show what life would be like in a land without root vegetables.

In the United States there was a similar drive to get people digging and gardening. The patriotic value of the enterprise was stressed by references to 'victory gardens', a term also used in Britain. American women were urged to tin and preserve the produce of their victory gardens, with a piece of ingenious Madison-Avenue sloganeering: 'Eat what you can, and can what you can't.'

*Line from a 'Dig for Victory' anthem often heard on the wireless. In its entirety, it ran: *Dig! Dig! Dig!/And your muscles will grow big/Keep on pushing the spade/Don't mind the worms/Just ignore their squirms/ And when your back aches laugh for glee /Just keep on digging/Till we give our foes a wigging/Dig! Dig Dig! for Victory!*

Loved and Loathed
[**American: Spam**®]

Well, there's egg and bacon; egg, sausage and bacon; egg and spam; egg, bacon and spam; egg, bacon, sausage and spam; spam, bacon, sausage and spam; spam, egg, spam, spam, bacon and spam; spam, sausage, spam, spam, bacon, spam, tomato and spam.

So shrieked Terry Jones in his trademark harridan's falsetto, in a *Monty Python's Flying Circus* sketch first broadcast in 1970. For its writers, Jones and Michael Palin, who grew up in Austerity Britain, the Spam Sketch was their characteristically manic revenge on the ubiquitous, nauseatingly pink luncheon meat that blighted many a fifties and sixties childhood. This three and a half minute skit not only became a surreal comedy classic but also, in the dawning IT age, gave the world a handy catch-all term for all the junk mail and other unsolicited advertising that washes about cyberspace. Small wonder there – early computer geeks were exactly the kind of people who could recite every last word of *Monty Python* from memory. And so 'spam' became a byword for omnipresent, instantly forgettable crap.

SPAM® ('spiced ham') is a precooked, canned pork product developed by the Hormel Foods Corporation of Austin, Minnesota ('Spam Town, USA') in 1937. It is preserved with sodium nitrite, and its long shelf life and easy transportability made it ideal for distribution both to troops and to civilians suffering from a lack of meat protein due to wartime rationing. It became an integral part of the 'K-ration' issued to American forces, where the myth soon arose that its name derived from 'special army meat'. Under the lend-lease programme, Spam was dispatched in vast quantities to America's allies, including Russia. Coincidentally, in the very same year the Pythons were driving the last nail into the coffin of Spam's reputation in the UK, Soviet premier Nikita Khrushchev recalled that: 'Without Spam we wouldn't have been able to feed our army.' And when it was first shipped to Britain in 1941, Spam was welcomed with open arms; it wasn't rationed and was – according to contributors to the BBC's 'People's War' online archive project – 'incredibly tasty' and 'an oasis in our desert of mediocrity'. Nor was it just besieged Britain that acquired a taste for it. World War Two and the Korean War saw the rubbery, jellified slab become a firm favourite across large swathes of the Pacific and Far East. The inhabitants of Hawaii, Guam and the Northern Mariana Islands became the largest per capita consumers in the world; Hawaiians alone now eat an average of six cans per person a year. It also remains a much-loved food in South Korea.

In Britain, its popularity waned with the rise of the affluent society. Philip Larkin famously claimed that sexual intercourse began in 1963, but the first inklings of that other great life-enhancing pleasure – good food – came to the British somewhat earlier, with the publication of Elizabeth David's *A Book of Mediterranean Food* in 1950. While old eating habits died hard, by 1970 Spam was decidedly infra dig for the middle classes and ripe for cruel mockery by sophisticated satirists. Lest we forget, though, Spam did sterling service in straitened times, and when all was said and done there was a range of far more unpalatable offerings available to nauseate the wartime gourmet.

Cat's Eyes and Carrolade
[British: 'Dr Carrot']

The British Ministry of Food was assiduous in its promotion of the carrot as a vital war-winning food. The plentiful supply of this healthy and nutritious root vegetable made it an ideal replacement for crops that were harder to grow or simply unavailable for the duration of the war. The challenge was to think up new ways of putting the humble vegetable to work, and the men and women from the ministry rose admirably to it, coming up with such culinary delights as curried carrot, carrot marmalade, carrot sandwiches and carrot jam. There was even something called 'carrolade', a drink made from the juices of carrot and swede, grated and pressed through muslin. The cartoon figure 'Dr Carrot' was invented in 1941; this cheery, rotund figure appeared on numerous posters with slogans such as 'Dr Carrot Will Protect You' and 'Dr Carrot the Children's Friend'.*

By way of popularising the carrot, British bureaucrats began spreading the rumour that the growing number of 'kills' of enemy bombers by British night-fighter pilots was due to their avid consumption of the vegetable. One ace in particular, Group Captain John Cunningham, was enlisted for this campaign, earning himself the nickname 'Cat's Eyes'. Enthralled, the general public began eating more carrots themselves. Yet the plain fact is that carrots do not improve night vision, although vitamin A, which they contain in abundance, certainly does help to keep eyes healthy. The ulterior motive for putting this story about was to conceal the real reason behind the RAF's success – developments in radar technology.

*A companion figure was 'Potato Pete'.

Disgusting Fare
[Italian: *'A.M.' (Amministrazione Militare)*, 'military authorities']

In an interesting parallel to the opprobrium heaped upon Spam by Allied forces and civilians, a form of 'bully beef' issued to Axis troops also attracted its fair share of savage mockery. The canned food in question, which had the initials 'A.M.' printed on the tin – short for *Amministrazione Militare*, or 'military authorities' – was produced as rations for Italian forces, but fell woefully short of the high standards of taste and quality normally associated with that country's cuisine. As Napoleon famously observed, an army marches on its stomach, and the food-loving Italians soon came up with various rude nicknames for this gristly, fatty, sinewy slop, including *asino morto* ('dead donkey') and *arabo morto* ('dead Arab'). German troops posted to Italy, Sicily or North Africa found their own disparaging terms, usually aimed at their less-than-revered ally, e.g. *armer Mussolini* ('poor Mussolini') or *Arsch Mussolini* ('Mussolini's arse'). But the most common, and rather sinister, German name for this unappetising fare appears in the online memoirs of the Afrika Korps veteran, Sergeant Helmuth Orschiedt:

> *22 June 1941 . . . then our diet, which was kind of dull: Dried vegetable soup, A.M.= Amministrazione Militare = tinned beef (we called it 'Alter Mann' = Old Man), tinned sardines, hard cheese . . .**

Orschiedt goes on to reveal that captured British rations were considered a delicacy, which speaks volumes about quite how awful 'A.M.' must have been.

*Science-fiction writer Philip K. Dick's 1962 counterfactual novel *The Man in the High Castle* makes mention of '*alter Mann*' and '*asino morte*' (*sic*).

Chapter 8

Coded Language: Abbreviations, Acronyms, Codewords and Operational Terms

If you travel along the A41 between Bicester and Aylesbury, you'll notice a clutch of red-bordered road signs bearing such inscriptions as 'DSDA/BOWMAN Centre/DCTA Caversfield' and which point, as it turns out, to British Army logistics facilities. The military has always been fond of acronyms that are gibberish to the rest of us. Even when coherent words do appear, they are used cryptically, chosen by heaven knows what rationale as the names of exercises, operations, secret agents and the like. Winston Churchill, as we shall see, had very decided views on this score. Latterly, Ben Macintyre's excellent histories (e.g. *Operation Mincemeat*, *Agent Zigzag*) have acquainted us with this world of military nomenclature. Here are our choice servings from the alphabet soup of World War Two.

Make it Snappy

[British/American: Military acronyms]

The practice of referring to people and things by an abbreviation or a pronounceable set of initials has existed for hundreds of years – SPQR, standing for *Senatus Populusque Romanus* ('the Senate and People of Rome') was, in effect, the logo of ancient Rome – but acronyms and abbreviations multiplied in the 20th century and the process was given a great boost by World War Two. It is no coincidence that the word 'acronym' itself, originating in the US, was first recorded in English in 1940 (it derives from the German *Akronym*). Of course, WW2/ II is itself a very familiar abbreviation or, technically speaking, an initialism. Another example is the title of what was probably the most significant military operation of the era, D-Day, although here the 'D' signifies nothing more than 'day'.

The need for speedy communication in wartime together with ease of reference are the principal reasons for the rise of the acronym, that is, a 'new' word formed out of the opening letters or syllables of a sequence of existing words. It was easier to say or to write CIGS or CINCPAC than to laboriously spell out the exalted positions which the letters stood for: respectively, Chief of the Imperial General Staff (for the British) and Commander-in-Chief US Pacific Fleet (for the Americans).

Some of the acronyms are peculiarly apt or have an almost euphonious quality. The pipeline laid under the English Channel to convey petrol to the French coast after the D-Day invasion was referred to as PLUTO (Pipe Line Under The Ocean). 'Seabees' were, and still are, the US Navy's Construction Battalions (or CBs), the engineers and builders of military airstrips, bridges, etc. The command centre for the Allied forces fighting in north-west Europe after June 1944 was SHAEF, standing for Supreme Headquarters Allied Expeditionary Force and pronounced 'shafe'. (Presumably it was a happy coincidence that this acronym, applied to the fighting forces of different nations bound together in common purpose, suggested 'sheaf' in its sound.)

The palindromic word RADAR was a US coinage, first suggested in 1940 and taken from the initial letters of 'radio detection and ranging'. The British equivalent, RDF (radio direction finding), was quickly superseded by the more catchy 'radar'. The need to search out hostile objects below the waves gave rise to ASDIC, for Allied Submarine Detection Investigation Committee, originally an Anglo-French organisation that, before the end of World War One, began to experiment with bouncing pulses of sound off submarine hulls. The US version is sonar, standing for sound navigation (and) ranging, and formed by analogy with radar.

Aside from radar, the most successful and enduring Allied acronym of the war was 'jeep'. This derived from the initials GP, in full 'general purpose', which was used to describe the unrestricted function of the vehicle. The attraction of a single-syllable word as against two longer words is obvious. Also, US troops would already have been familiar with Eugene Jeep, the name of a dog-like creature possessing magical powers who appeared in the *Popeye* cartoon strips from the mid-1930s. Despite the almost homely nature of this acronym, the jeep was reckoned by General Eisenhower to be one of the three tools that won the war for the Allies, the others being the Dakota aircraft and landing craft.

The US's most universal export, in several senses, was the initialism G.I., defining the ordinary soldier who, in later wars like Vietnam, became a 'grunt'. As with the equally universal expression OK, there is no agreement about what G.I. actually stands for. The most immediate derivation is 'Government Issue', since even before America entered the war the supplies issued to troops were referred to in this style (G.I. soap, G.I. shoes, G.I. trucks) and it is easy to see how the recipients of such a range of equipment would soon start to refer to themselves as G.I.s. But before that G.I. stood for 'galvanised iron'. Thus a 'G.I. can/boiler' was an iron cooking pot used by the US army in the 1930s. And even earlier, during World War One, the same phrase, G.I. cans, was slang for German artillery shells because of their likeness to the galvanised bins (ash cans) from civilian life. Whatever its derivation, G.I. was the widely used abbreviation for the ordinary serviceman by the time America entered the war, often coupled with another standard US colloquialism in 'G.I. Joe'. You couldn't get more normal or representative than that.

The Semantics of Secrecy

[German: WOTAN/*Freya Gerät* (Freya Apparatus)]

Winston Churchill had firm views on how military operations should be named. They are worth quoting in full not only because of their humorous good sense but because they indicate some of the pitfalls which careless code-naming could produce. In a minute dated 8 August 1943 to General Ismay, Churchill's liaison with the Chiefs of Staff, he wrote:

Operations in which large numbers of men may lose their lives ought not to be decided by code-words that imply a boastful and over-confident sentiment, such as

'Triumphant', or conversely, which are calculated to invest the plan with an air of despondency, such as 'Woebetide' and 'Flimsy'. They ought not to be names of a frivolous character, such as 'Bunnyhug' and 'Ballyhoo'. They should not be ordinary words often used in other connections, such as 'Flood', 'Sudden', and 'Supreme'. Names of living people – ministers or commanders – should be avoided. Intelligent thought will already supply an unlimited number of well-sounding names that do not suggest the character of the operation or disparage it in any way and do not enable some widow or mother to say that her son was killed in an operation called 'Bunnyhug' or 'Ballyhoo'. Proper names are good in this field. The heroes of antiquity, figures from Greek and Roman mythology, the constellations and stars, famous race-horses, names of British and American war heroes, could be used, provided they fall within the rules above.

The unintentionally revealing nature of a code name worked to British advantage when, in 1940, the Enigma decoding operation based at Bletchley Park deciphered a reference to a WOTAN installation being set up on the French coast. It was apparent that this was connected to radar, but the reference to the ancient Germanic god Wotan or Woden (who gives his name to Wednesday) was enough to make the boffin R.V. Jones telephone a fellow academic to ask what was significant about this particular deity. As Jones recalled in *Most Secret War* (1978):

. . . he replied 'Yes, he was Head of the German Gods . . . Wait a moment . . . He had only one eye.' And then,

shouting triumphantly into the telephone, 'ONE EYE –
ONE BEAM! Can you think of a system that would use
only one beam?' I replied that I could, for in principle one
could have the bomber fly along a beam pointing over the
target, and have something like a radar station alongside
the beam transmitter so that the distance of the bomber
could be continuously measured from the starting point
of the beam. A controller there could know both the
distance of the bomber from its target and its speed, from
which he could work out the correct instant at which the
aircraft should release its bombs to hit the target.

R.V. Jones also deduced that a German code name *Freya*
Gerät (Freya Apparatus) might refer to a chain of radar instal-
lations, since the goddess Freya's most prized possession was a
necklace. This he learned from a book on Norse mythology
purchased at Foyle's. With dry wit, Jones also noted a connection between Wotan and Freya, who was his mistress, adding
that when it came to code names one might expect that: 'the
Führer would have in this case chosen Frigga, who was Wotan's
lawful wife.'

Condemned Out of their Own Mouths
[German: *Eichhörnchen, Streichholzschächtelchen,*
'squirrel', 'matchbox' – tongue-twisters
to catch out Allied spies]

The Old Testament Book of Judges (chapter 12, verses 5–6)
records the fate of the tribe of Ephraim in retreat following
their unsuccessful assault on the region of Gilead:

And so the Gileadites took the passages of Jordan before the Ephraimites; and it was so that when those Ephraimites which were escaped said Let me go over; that the men of Gilead said unto them: Art thou an Ephraimite? And if he say, Nay; Then say unto him, Say now Shibboleth: and he said Sibboleth; for he could not frame to pronounce it right. Then they took him and slew him at the passages of Jordan . . .

History abounds with instances of the 'enemy within' betraying themselves through their inability to pronounce certain words or phrases that tripped easily off the native tongue. During World War Two, so claims the *vox pop* of the Internet, German spies in Britain were caught out by 'squirrel'; in fact, the idea of this word as a surefire way of smoking out Teutons in our midst was first mooted by Jeremy Clarkson on a 2007 episode of 'Top Gear'. True enough, Germans do struggle with the English 'qu', turning it into a 'kv' sound, but there would have been little need for such an offbeat term as an acid test when a much easier pitfall lay in that commonest of words, the definite article 'the'. The English phoneme 'th' habitually ties in knots the tongues not just of Germans but most of the rest of the non-Anglophone world, too.

By a curious linguistic coincidence, though, there is evidence to suggest that the German word for 'squirrel', *Eichhörnchen*, was indeed used as a shibboleth to entrap spies or escaped POWs. Pronouncing this demands labial acrobatics that are beyond many otherwise proficient English speakers of German. The problem lies not only in the repeated 'ch' consonant (a soft sound more at home in the Scots mouth, approximating to the endings of the Gaelic words 'pibroch' or 'sassenach') but also in the tricky umlauted 'ö' in between. An even more severe test was posed by *Streichholzschächtelchen* ('matchbox'). Try getting your gums round that, Clarkson.

There are also two well-known and authentic examples of Dutch–German shibboleths from World War Two. At root, Dutch is a dialect of Low German (conversely, 'Dutch' and 'Deutsch' are cognate, with many older English primers of the German language referring to it as 'High Dutch'). Nevertheless, many sounds are only truly accessible to Dutch natives: the notoriously difficult names of the towns of 'Scheveningen' and 'Nijmegen' were used to unmask Nazi spies and German soldiers disguised as civilians fleeing Holland in 1945.

Scourge of the East?

**[German: *Fall Barbarossa*,
'Case (= Operation) Barbarossa']**

Anyone with even a passing interest in World War Two knows that the German attack on Soviet Russia in June 1941 was code-named 'Barbarossa'. Hitler made his intentions plain, and christened his plan, in the famous *Führer-Weisung* ('Führer Directive') No. 21 of 18 December 1940:

> *The German Armed Forces must make preparations to overrun Soviet Russia in a rapid campaign even before the war against England has been brought to a close (Case Barbarossa).*

The *Wehrmacht* commanders and others who had sight of this order would have immediately understood the import of the name. Ever since 1871, when German unification came about under the aegis of Prussia and the Second German Empire was founded, a nationalistic cult had grown up around the most famous ruler of the first 'German' empire – the Holy Roman Empire – Frederick I ('Barbarossa', r. 1152–90). One notable achievement of this Hohenstaufen monarch's reign was the gradual eastward settlement and Germanisation of the regions of Silesia and Pomerania, formerly home to West Slavic peoples.

Long after his death, Barbarossa became the subject of a legend which claimed that he was not dead but sleeping in a cave inside a mountain, waiting to return in glory to reclaim his throne and bring his country eternal peace. The site in question – at 453 metres above sea level, more a hill than a mountain – was the Kyffhäuser on the southern fringes of the Harz Mountains. In order to legitimise the Second Empire's claim to historical continuity, a grand monument was erected on the summit in 1896, depicting Barbarossa waking from his centuries-long slumber, surmounted by an equestrian statue of the recently deceased Prussian emperor Wilhelm I (r. 1871–88). The impetus for the construction of this hideous sandstone and bronze lump came from a war veterans' association, the *Deutscher Kriegerbund* ('German Warriors' Federation').

All these powerful martial and nationalistic resonances made 'Barbarossa' the obvious choice for Hitler when naming his grandiose plan to seize *Lebensraum* to the east and eliminate Bolshevism. Perhaps he should have delved beyond the myth before committing himself, however: it was on Barbarossa's most ambitious eastern adventure, the Third Crusade, that he came to an ignominious end, drowning in his heavy armour as he tried to cross the Saleph River (modern name: Göksu) in Anatolia.

Clued In

[British: The 'D-Day' crosswords]

One of the odder coincidences of World War Two occurred when a trail of significant clues, or rather answers, appeared in *Daily Telegraph* crosswords during the run-up to D-Day on 6 June 1944. In May, the answer 'Utah', clued by 'One of the USA', followed references in previous months to Juno, Gold and Sword, and then on 22 May came the clue 'Red Indian on the Missouri (5)' to which the answer was 'Omaha'. The next few days saw the appearance of Overlord, Mulberry and, finally, Neptune. Thus were revealed the code names of all five of the Normandy beaches where assault forces were to land, together with the code name for the entire invasion (Overlord), the naval assault itself (Neptune) and the system of floating harbours (Mulberry).

Was this sheer coincidence or the work of traitors or spies? MI5 was alarmed enough to question the crossword compilers. As Leonard Dawe, headmaster of a school in Surrey during the war, recalled in a 1958 BBC interview:

> *They turned me inside out. They went to Bury St Edmunds where my senior colleague Melville Jones (the paper's other crossword compiler) was living and put him through the works. But they eventually decided not to shoot us after all.*

It took more than twenty years for the likely solution to the D-Day crossword puzzles to emerge. Dawe's school was close to where American and Canadian troops were quartered in preparation for the invasion. As headmaster, he sometimes gave empty crossword grids to his sixth-formers to fill in as a mental exercise, after which he would create clues for the words they'd supplied. And, in those heady pre-invasion days, a few of those same boys enjoyed the thrill of hanging around the army camp. One even recalled being allowed to drive a tank. They also picked up the chatter – and a few code names – from soldiers who knew the names without knowing the locations.

Leonard Dawe and the *Daily Telegraph* had form when it came to secret operations and crosswords. Immediately before the large-scale raid on Dieppe harbour of 19 August 1942, the crossword featured the clue 'French port' and the solution 'Dieppe' on successive days. It was perhaps the disastrous outcome of this precursor to D-Day, in which over 3,000 troops were killed, wounded or captured, which prompted an exhaustive enquiry into whether the crossword, again the work of Leonard Dawe, had revealed the secret target of the raid. In the end it was concluded that it was 'just a remarkable coincidence – a complete fluke'.

Crosswords were a relatively new and popular diversion in wartime so MI5 was right to be suspicious. Passing on coded messages in newspapers had been a favourite device of crime and thriller fiction from Sherlock Holmes to Agatha Christie. Meanwhile, aficionados of the crossword will note that the D-Day clues are of the straight, non-cryptic variety (i.e. they simply define the word required in the solution – 'French port' – rather than providing additional word play such as an anagram).

A Corporal and a Dauber

[**German:** *der böhmische Gefreite,*
'the Bohemian corporal'; *Der Anstreicher,*
'the dauber, the (house-) painter']

As much of the contemporary newsreel footage and stills photography clearly shows, millions of Germans and Austrians were in thrall to Adolf Hitler, mesmerised by his steel-blue eyes and entranced by his hectoring style of oratory. But there were plenty of nay-sayers, too, and over the course of his rise and fall, some disparaging nicknames were coined for the Führer.

Traditional conservatives in Weimar Germany – chief among them Hitler's predecessor as chancellor, Franz von Papen of the Centre Party – fatally underestimated the leader of the NSDAP, regarding him as an upstart who could be kept in check and manipulated. Von Papen's close political confederate Paul von Hindenburg gave voice to their lofty aristocratic disdain for this ranting demagogue when, on 10 October 1931, he referred to Hitler as '*der böhmische Gefreite*', 'the Bohemian corporal'.* Not only should Hitler's alarming rise have commanded more respect from the former Prussian Field Marshal (this was barely a year after the Nazis had gained 107 seats in the Reichstag, up from just 12 in 1928), but Hindenburg also betrayed his failing grasp on reality by getting his facts wrong. Hitler was from Braunau in Austria, which the 84-year old Hindenburg confused with Braunau in the predominantly German-speaking area of Czechoslovakia known as the Sudetenland (the town is now Broumov in the Czech Republic).

To each his own: whereas the Right lighted upon Hitler's

lowly rank in the Bavarian Army during World War One to try and belittle him, the Left chose to mock a failed ambition from an even earlier period of his life. From 1905 to 1913, the young Adolf Hitler lived in Vienna, eking out a living as a casual labourer while trying to achieve his main goal, entry to the Academy of Fine Arts. He applied twice, in 1907 and 1908, but was turned down due to his patent lack of talent. His watercolours from this period (which now command huge sums at auction from memorabilia collectors) are of mainly architectural subjects, painstakingly but ineptly copied from picture postcards. Alluding to Hitler as a painter *manqué*, in several poems dating from 1933 onwards the Marxist play-wright and poet Bertolt Brecht called him '*Der Anstreicher*'. When applied to someone with designs on becoming a *Kunstmaler* (i.e. a fine artist), this term means a 'dauber'. But in general usage it denotes a painter and decorator, a trade famously portrayed in Robert Tressell's socialist novel *The Ragged-Trousered Philanthropists* (1911). So, Brecht's insult sounded for all the world like he was doing down a form of honest toil rather than sneering at Hitler's pretensions (Hitler never was a house-painter, incidentally). Albeit for a very different reason, this was as much an own goal as Hindenburg's attempted put-down. The myth of Hitler as a decorator was eagerly picked up by the Allies: a British wartime propaganda film encouraging people to donate rolls of unused wallpaper to the war effort had an actor doing a crude impersonation of Hitler and the legend: 'Every scrap of paper you save can help hang the paper hanger!' A lapel badge with the same sentiment was produced in the US, and in Mel Brooks's scurrilous and hugely funny film *The Producers* (1968), the leading man in the ultimate bad-taste Nazi-themed musical 'Springtime for

Hitler' sings: 'I was just a paper hanger/no one more obscurer/ Got a 'phone call from the Reichstag/told me I was Führer.'

*A 'whispered joke' (*see* Chapter 11: Laughter in the Dark) that did the rounds later in the war imagined Hitler visiting the *Tannenbergdenkmal*, the monument in East Prussia marking the site of Hindenburg's great victory over the Russians in 1914, and lamenting in rhyme: *O Hindenburg, du großer Streiter,/Hier steht ein Gefreiter,/ Und kann nicht weiter!* ('O Hindenburg, you great warrior, here stands a corporal who is at his wits' end).

Short but not so Sweet
[British/American: Spoof acronyms]

While many abbreviations and acronyms were simply functional – MIA for missing in action or sitrep for situation report, for example – the process had a comic side and also a clumsy one. Not every item of equipment or rank or system could be reduced to the snappy poetry of the jeep or a PLUTO or the neat initialism of the G.I. The US Commander of the Amphibious Force in the South Pacific was designated by the lumbering COMAMPHIBFORSOPAC, while the acronym for the organisation set up by SHAEF in 1945 to trace war criminals was CROWCASS (Central Registry of War Criminals and Security Suspects). And there was always the possibility that an innocent string of letters would turn out to mean something quite different in another language. Such was the case with AMGOT or the American Military Government of Occupied Territories. Alarm bells soon rang in the highest quarters. Winston Churchill sent a query to an official in the Foreign Office: 'Could you find out for me whether the word *Amgot* in Turkish means camel's dung or something equally unpleasant?'

In fact, it translates, roughly, as 'arsehole'. The War Department shortened the offending initials to AMG.

But many, if not most, of the official acronyms and abbreviations employed on all fronts during World War Two would have meant nothing to those outside those areas. This is, in itself, one of the functions of the acronym. Rather like jargon and some types of slang, its use confers a little bit of status on insiders, confirming their membership of the group and excluding those who aren't in the know.

There was also a healthy tendency to subvert authority and efficiency by twisting existing acronyms away from their purpose or even inventing entirely new ones. Such distortions pointed to the gap between appearance and reality, between the way *they* pretended things were and the actual experience of ordinary men and women caught up in the war, i.e. almost everyone. Some of the British alternative acronyms had an almost innocent quality. The sometimes low standard of entertainment provided for troops by actors, singers, musicians, etc. under the direction of the Entertainment National Service Association (ENSA) meant that the initials were said to stand for 'Every Night Something Awful'. ENSA itself was controlled by the NAAFI, the Navy, Army and Airforce Institutes, which ran canteens, bars, shops and other welfare services for the armed forces. At least two alternative interpretations sprang up: 'Never 'Ave Any Fags In' and 'No Ambition And Fuck-all Interest'.

Among initial abbreviations, LDV was the short-lived title for the Local Defence Volunteers or the Home Guard as they soon became. But they were also known as the Look, Duck and Vanish Brigade, not least to themselves. Away from the Home Front, the British Expeditionary Force (BEF) – the term used in both world wars for the British forces fighting in Europe – endured such a long run of retreats and evacuations, including those from Dunkirk, Greece and Crete, that the initials were said to stand for 'back every fortnight' or 'back every Friday'. Even the elevated matter of gong-giving wasn't immune from satirical reduction. Among other decorations introduced in 1917 to honour individuals who had contributed to the war (World War One) effort but were not eligible for bravery awards were the OBE and the MBE, both referring to the glory days of the British Empire but soon jokingly transmuted into Other Buggers'/Bastards' Efforts and Measly Bleeding Effort (or sometimes My Bloody Effort). On a milder note, the wildly popular radio comedy programme ITMA, standing for It's That Man Again, was responsible for several catchphrases, including TTFN or 'Ta-ta for now'. As noted above Winston Churchill was in the habit of ending phone calls with his private maxim KBO or Keep Buggering On, to the occasional confusion of his listeners.

Some of the invented acronyms, especially those coined in the US, carried a more aggressive edge. It may be that the more egalitarian spirit of American society contributed to an instinctive distrust of hierarchy, even in the military. An apocryphal story circulated about the tough and foul-mouthed US general, George S. Patton, who while inspecting a hospital in France encountered a man who did not snap to attention in his presence. Patton went ballistic. The man patiently waited out his tirade before replying: 'Run along, asshole. I'm in the Merchant Marine.' An acronym equivalent was FUBID or 'Fuck You Buddy, I'm Detached' while someone whose tour of duty was ending might respond to any request with FUBIS, the last two letters standing for 'I'm Shipping [out]'. It is the same spirit of non-compliance and passive resistance which informs Joseph Heller's classic anti-war satire *Catch-22* (1961).

The universality of the f-word produced a little tree of acronyms, all the branches growing out of a common trunk, with the two standard ones being SNAFU (Situation Normal, All Fucked Up) and FUBAR (Fucked Up Beyond All Recognition). Both of these were American in origin and while it was possible to euphemise the 'F' as standing for 'Fouled' everyone knew what was really meant. Variants included TARFU (Things Are Really . . .), FUBB (. . . Beyond Belief), GFU (General . . .), SUSFU (Situation Unchanged Still . . .) and TULFU (The Ultimate In . . .). This is far from exhausting the list, even if some of the FU acronyms have a rather contrived air.

More poignant as well as raunchy acronyms might be found at the end of the letters* sent by servicemen to their wives and girlfriends at home. SWALK (sealed with a loving kiss) is the most familiar, although it first appeared in the less enthusiastic form of SWAK many years before the outbreak of World War Two, while BURMA (be undressed ready, my angel) has been traced back as far as the 19th century. More certainly dated to the 1940s are three from various points on the romantic/lust spectrum: ITALY (I trust and love you), HOLLAND (here our love lies and never dies) and NORWICH ([k]nickers off ready when I come home).

*Letters sent the other way sometimes contained the unwelcome news that a wife or girlfriend had found someone else and wanted to break things off. For the G.I.s these became known as 'Dear John' letters. According to an item in a New York State newspaper in August 1945: '"Dear John," the letter began. "I have found someone else whom I think the world of. I think the only way out is for us to get a divorce," it said. They usually began like that, those letters that told of infidelity on the part of the wives of servicemen.' These communications were familiar enough for the opening to be compressed into a single word, 'dearjohn'. An equivalent letter in the Pacific war was a Green Banana, presumably because these were hard to swallow, but it is debatable how far that term caught on.

The Compliment that Backfired

[German: *der größte Feldherr aller Zeiten (GröFaZ),* 'the Greatest Commander of All Time']

Following Nazi Germany's victory in the rapid armoured thrust (*Blitzkrieg*) against the Low Countries and France in May–June 1940, Field Marshal Wilhelm Keitel,* Chief of the Supreme Command of the Armed Forces, hailed Hitler in the following terms:

> *Mein Führer, Sie sind der größte Feldherr aller Zeiten . . .*
> (My Führer, you are the greatest commander of all time.)

But after the disastrous Battle of Stalingrad, this term of adulation – now abbreviated to the acronym 'GröFaZ' – began to be used ironically. Hitler had ordered General Friedrich Paulus, commanding the Sixth Army at Stalingrad, to fight to the last man and appointed him a Field Marshal as the battle neared its end in January/February 1943. He expected Paulus, who would have been well aware that no German officer of this rank had ever been taken prisoner, to fall on his sword. In the event, Paulus surrendered and he and over 90,000 of his men went into a long captivity from which all but some 6,000 never returned. The 'greatest commander of all time' had precipitated the worst defeat in German military history.

In the wake of this catastrophe, many former followers of the Führer – army officers who had supported him in his aggressive seizure of *Lebensraum* – grew increasingly restive. The sneering contempt implicit in the term 'GröFaZ' grew to a point where, on 20 July 1944, an attempt was made on Hitler's life. The conspirators were, principally, aristocratic elements within the upper echelons of the Wehrmacht, a caste which, at root, had always resented being commanded by the Austrian corporal (*see* A Corporal and a Dauber). Keitel, though, remained loyal to the last, sitting on the army court that condemned the plotters, and finally signing the unconditional surrender of the German Army at a ceremony in Berlin on 8 May 1945. He was found guilty of war crimes at Nuremberg and hanged in October 1946.

*Keitel's extreme obsequiousness towards Hitler earned him the nickname 'Lackeitel', a conflation of his name with the word *Lackei* (= 'lackey, crawler').

The Red Tsar

[**Russian/American:** Stalin/Uncle Joe/*Vozhd*]

The Soviet leader Joseph Stalin had several nicknames and assumed names, beginning with Stalin itself. Born Iosif Dzhugashvíli, he early on considered the alias Stalin ('[man of] steel') to be more suitable for his role. In the West, Stalin was referred to as 'Uncle Joe', both in himself and as the personification of Soviet communism. There was an uncomfortable moment at the Yalta summit conference in 1945 when Stalin took offence on learning that President Roosevelt and Churchill referred to him in telegrams as 'Uncle Joe'. The tension was only defused when an American member of the negotiating group said: 'After all, you do not mind talking about Uncle Sam, so why should Uncle Joe be so bad?' There might have been something avuncular about Uncle Joe but his embrace was more to be feared than loved. In the same way as George Orwell drew upon the resonance of Winston Churchill's name when creating a hero for *Nineteen Eighty-Four*, so he used the sinisterly reassuring figure of Josef Stalin in his invention of Big Brother, the all-seeing, all-knowing head of state who never appears as anything but an image and who may not even exist: '. . . the face of Big Brother, black-haired, black-moustachio'd, full of power and mysterious calm, and so vast that it almost filled up the screen.' Russians respectfully referred to Stalin as *Vozhd*, simply meaning 'leader'.

Winston and the Cross He had to Bear

[British/French: Winnie/*Deux Mètres* (Two Metres)]

As with some other successful and charismatic political leaders, Winston Churchill's first name alone was enough to identify him. On Sunday, 3 September 1939, the day that war was declared, the 64-year-old Churchill was appointed First Lord of the Admiralty, a return to the post that he had held in the early part of World War One. Out went the signal from Whitehall to the Royal Navy, complete with exclamation mark: 'Winston is back!' For the general public Churchill was 'Winnie' and welcomed as a hero, especially during the Blitz. As the *Australian Sunday Times* reported in February 1941: 'Greeted with shouts of "Good Old Winnie," British Premier (Mr Winston Churchill) told Portsmouth and Southampton dockers, "We shall come through."' The affectionate diminutive spread across the Atlantic and it was as 'Winnie' that he was familiar to the American public.

Assisted by his jowly features, growling tones and combative nature, Churchill cultivated the bulldog image, and it may have been the Russians who first termed him the 'British Bulldog'. This image can be conflated with that of John Bull, originally a satirical depiction of the English spirit, and referring to a bull rather than the bulldog sometimes envisaged by later generations. The name Winston continued to resonate after the war, and it is no coincidence that George Orwell chose it for his heroic, but doomed, protagonist in *Nineteen Eighty-Four* (1949), just as he chose to make him Winston Smith, thus yoking together the forename of the most famous living Englishman with the most common and recognisable of English surnames. Churchill enjoyed communicating with the American President, Franklin Delano Roosevelt, under the code name of 'former naval person'.* It was an in-joke allusion to his time at the Admiralty, but Roosevelt's nickname was nothing more elaborate than his initials, FDR.

The founder of the Free French forces, General Charles de Gaulle, was an awkward, prickly figure, acutely conscious of his position as a leader who was almost entirely dependent on the goodwill of the British and Americans for as long as he was in exile from his own country. In the run-up to D-Day, de Gaulle was furious at being excluded from the invasion planning and at the reluctance of the US to acknowledge him as head of the provisional government of France. In the event, he made a triumphal entry into Paris on 26 August 1944. To senior Americans, the 6 foot 5 inch French leader was known as *Deux Mètres* (a variant on a long-standing French nickname for him, *Double Mètre*). Less respectfully, the recurring stresses of de Gaulle's relationship with Churchill gave the British Prime Minister critical material for what he referred to as his 'Frog File'. More wittily, de Gaulle was also referred to as Churchill's 'Cross of Lorraine', and though the phrase is sometimes attributed to him it was actually the punning invention of the British general who accompanied de Gaulle across the Channel after the fall of France in 1940.

*When he travelled to summit conferences, Churchill usually employed a pseudonym; his assumed names included Colonel Warden, Mr Lobb (after John Lobb, the still-thriving London company which made the Prime Minister's shoes) and Colonel Kent (an allusion to his country home at Chartwell?). Although there were good reasons of security and secrecy for the adoption of false names like these, there is no doubt that they would have appealed to the boyish and buoyant side of Churchill's adventurous nature. Nor were his pseudonyms confined to war work. As a painter, he exhibited in Paris in 1921 as Charles Morin, and sold four landscapes for £30, while after the war he submitted two paintings to the Royal Academy under the name of Mr Winter.

Chapter 9

Military Hardware

Though coined by the distinguished wartime commander Dwight D. Eisenhower, the phrase 'military–industrial complex' was used by him for the first time only when stepping down as US President in 1961. But it was during World War Two above all that centrally planned mass-production of armaments and other war materiel proved decisive to the outcome of the conflict. The industrial might of the United States and the huge pool of manpower (and womanpower) available to the USSR – in factories which, in many cases, had been dismantled and moved east, away from the invading Germans, to safety beyond the Urals – were overwhelming.

'A Drink to go with the Food'

[Finnish: *Molotohvin koktaili*, 'Molotov cocktail']

Stalin's Foreign Minister was like his master in adopting a name which signified he was not to be taken lightly. While Iosif Dzhugashvíli turned himself into the '[man of] steel' or Stalin, Vyacheslav Skriabin took on the name of Molotov or 'hammer'. An early member of the Politburo with a reputation as a tireless negotiator, he was nicknamed 'iron arse' or 'stone bottom' by Lenin.

Molotov was responsible for the Soviet drive against Finland during the 'Winter War' of 1939–40 and in a speech at the start of the campaign he claimed that his country would be bringing bread and not bombs to the Finns. It was inevitable, then, that the containers of multiple incendiary bombs which were actually dropped should become known sarcastically as 'Molotov breadbaskets'. Among the recipients these devices were sometimes also called 'Nolotovs', because the Finnish word '*nolo*' refers to a stupid or hapless individual. In response to the 'breadbaskets', Finnish fighters provided what they called 'a drink to go with the food', in the form of bottles filled with petrol and tar flung at the Russian tanks. Christened 'Molotov cocktails', these were produced by the country's monopoly alcohol corporation, Alko, and were considered effective enough as an improvised weapon against armoured forces for the Home Guard in Britain to adopt them in preparation for a German invasion.

On the international stage, the Commissar for Foreign Affairs gave his name to the non-aggression treaty signed by him and the German Foreign Minister in August 1939 (the Molotov–Ribbentrop Pact), which allowed Hitler to concentrate his attentions towards the West before his ultimately catastrophic decision to turn on the Soviet Union. Molotov, who was the only senior figure on the Allied side to have met Hitler, was in at the very beginning of the Russian Revolution; he was there almost to the end, dying in 1986, three years before the fall of the Berlin Wall.

A Terrible Prophecy

[British: 'Sow the Wind, Reap the Whirlwind']

The first of the 'Thousand-Bomber Raids' flown by the Royal

Air Force in World War Two took place on 30–31 May 1942. Its target was the Rhineland city of Cologne. Three days later the head of Bomber Command, Air Chief Marshal Arthur Harris, sat in front of an RAF newsreel crew and delivered a speech entitled 'Strategic Offensive Against Germany', which has become infamous for a particular phrase. In assessing the raid, and alluding to the Luftwaffe's attacks on cities such as Coventry and London, Harris declared:

They have sown the wind, and now they are going to reap the whirlwind.

There is a poetic resonance to this utterance not usually associated with military men; in fact, it is a quotation from the Old Testament Book of Hosea, chapter 8, verse 7. Harris was clearly pleased with his meteorological metaphor, for he continued:

Cologne, Lübeck, Rostock – those are only just the beginning ... when the storm bursts over Germany, they will look back to the days of Lübeck and Rostock and Cologne as a man caught in the blasts of a hurricane will look back to the gentle zephyrs of last summer.

The air marshal acknowledged that the area bombing of cities had never been tried before on the scale he was planning, so he can have had only a scant idea of just how appallingly literal his figurative turn of phrase was about to become. On the night of 27–28 July 1943, a huge raid was launched against the port of Hamburg. The attackers' intention was clear – in another Biblical reference, it was code-named 'Operation Gomorrah', the Canaanite city that suffered the 'vengeance of eternal fire'.

To start with, 4,000-lb high-explosive bombs were dropped to blast open the doors and windows of buildings. These were followed by small incendiaries to ignite roofs and larger fire-bombs to penetrate basements and set them ablaze. The resulting conflagration rapidly grew so intense that it began to generate its own wind system (a phenomenon physicists call the 'stack effect'). Within just twenty minutes of the raid starting, Hamburg was engulfed in a firestorm. W.G. Sebald's lecture *Air War and Literature* (1999) gives a compelling account of the unfolding tragedy:

> *The fire, now rising 2,000 metres into the sky, snatched oxygen to itself so violently that the air currents reached hurricane force, resonating like mighty organs with all their stops pulled out at once . . . At its height the storm lifted gables and roofs from buildings, flung rafters and entire advertising hoardings through the air, tore trees from the ground and drove human beings before it like living torches.*

A whirlwind indeed – sweeping away an estimated 40,000 souls like so many tinder-dry leaves caught in a gale.

Foiled Again
[American/British: Chaff/Window]

Chaff is the worthless part of corn or other grain, the husks which are separated in threshing. It's also a rather dated term applied to mild ridicule, possibly because of some shared sense of lightness. The same word was used by the US Army Air

Force during World War Two for the strips of metal foil released during bombing raids as a distracting countermeasure against enemy radar. The presence of the incoming aircraft was hidden or blurred by the overwhelming effect of the chaff. Used on a large scale for the first time during a series of raids on Hamburg in the summer of 1943 (see above), chaff resulted in a reduction of about three-quarters in the rate of loss for the bombers. This was a very cost-effective piece of deception. A few ounces of the metallic strips were said to provide a radar reflection equivalent to that of three heavy bombers.

It's easy to see why the USAAF came up with 'chaff' for these clusters of tiny, floating objects. Less obvious is the British equivalent for the same thing: Window. Perhaps this code name, the creation of a radar scientist, was intended ironically, since the use of 'Window' made it almost impossible for the enemy to 'see' where you were. Or perhaps it refers indirectly to the reflective quality of a real window. There is no connection with later quasi-military expressions such as 'window of opportunity' or 'window of vulnerability'. The Germans developed their own version of chaff/Window which they called Düppel, after the suburb of Berlin where it was developed.

Eccentric but Effective
[British: Hobart's Funnies]

On 19 October 1940, Churchill sent a memo to the Chief of the Imperial General Staff, Sir John Dill, speaking in glowing terms about one of his subordinates:

I was very much pleased last week when you told me you proposed to give an armoured division to Major-General Hobart. I think very highly of this officer, and I am not at all impressed by the prejudices against him in certain quarters. Such prejudices attach frequently to persons of strong personality and original view.

At the time when Churchill penned his fulsome note, Percy Cleghorn Stanley Hobart, formerly of the Royal Engineers, was a lance-corporal in the Home Guard, having been sent into retirement by General Archibald Wavell when he took command of the Middle East, where Hobart was serving. Just as tank specialist Charles de Gaulle had done in the interwar French army, Hobart put forward outspoken and unconventional ideas about mechanised warfare and got up the noses of his more line-toeing superiors.

Churchill's confidence was not misplaced. Initially, 'Hobo' did a good job reorganising a conventional tank division. Then, after a disastrous Allied assault on Dieppe in 1942 cruelly exposed the shortcomings of regular tanks and infantry in trying to seize a fortified beach, he took charge of the 79th Armoured Division, with orders to transform it into a specialised unit. There, using existing tank types as his basic material, he set about creating some of the strangest engines of war the world has ever seen.

They included the Scorpion and Crab flail tanks, which had a revolving drum the width of the vehicle mounted forward of the tracks and equipped with heavy chains. When the drum was set spinning, the chains lashed into the ground to a depth of nine inches, detonating buried anti-personnel mines. Another was the Crocodile, a flame-throwing tank towing an armoured trailer of fuel (an early form of napalm), which could direct a stream of liquid fire 120 yards through the slits of pillboxes and gun emplacements. Assault vehicles were also designed to carry bridging equipment like short box-girder bridges, or fascines (large bundles of poles or brushwood) to fill in ditches; one tank, called the ARK, had flat ramps in place of a turret and could drive up to a sheer escarpment and extend its ramps, thus forming a slope that allowed other vehicles to drive over the top of it and surmount the obstacle. In addition, in order to bring armoured fire-power to bear as quickly as possible on the coastal defences, Hobart applied an ingenious tank flotation device designed by a Hungarian emigré engineer, Nicholas Straussler. The 'Duplex Drive' (DD) system allowed propulsion to be switched from the tracks to a set of propellers, while the tank's hull above the tracks was sealed in a watertight screen made of rubberised canvas that was raised on launching and lowered when the tank reached dry land. Crews rechristened the amphibious DDs 'Donald Ducks'. Collectively, this odd assortment of mechanical monsters became known as 'Hobart's Funnies'.

The Americans were offered a third of the stock of these special-purpose vehicles, but General Omar Bradley, commanding US invasion forces, was loath to spend time retraining his men on unfamiliar tank types, and only accepted the DD variant of the American M4 Sherman tank. Even then, all but five of the 32 Sherman DDs deployed at Omaha Beach sank, their flotation screens swamped by heavy swell as a result of being launched too far from shore in seas that were too rough. The terrible difficulty experienced by US forces in consolidating a beachhead there and at their other landing site at Utah Beach has been attributed in part to Bradley's reluctance to use the full range of Hobart's Funnies.

Herr Meier's Empty Boast

[**German:** *Vergeltungswaffen,*
'retribution weapons'/'V-weapons']

Among the Allies, 'V' denoted 'Victory' (*see* Chapter 3: 'V' for Victory), whereas in Hitler's Germany it stood for *Vergeltung* (meaning 'revenge', 'repayment' or 'retribution'). As the war dragged on and the German civilian populace suffered ever-greater privations, the Nazi propaganda machine increasingly used this term in a series of buzzwords (e.g. *Vergeltungsangriff*, 'reprisal raid'; *Vergeltungsschlag*, 'retaliatory strike') designed to signal that the fight was being taken to the enemy. Undoubtedly the most famous of these 'V' compounds was *Vergeltungswaffen* ('reprisal weapon'), applied to the long-range V-1 and V-2 missiles launched primarily against England from June 1944 to March 1945.*

Revenge for what? The obvious answer, and the one peddled by the regime's propagandists, was the carpet-bombing of German cities, which over the entire course of the war cost the lives of around 600,000 civilians and destroyed some three and a half million homes (figures from the novelist W.G. Sebald's 1999 work *Luftkrieg und Literatur*, 'Air War and Literature') see A Terrible Prophecy. Some of these attacks were truly devastating: on the night of 27–28 July 1943, a mass raid on Hamburg caused a firestorm in which tens of thousands of citizens died (*see* A Terrible Prophecy).

Yet given the Nazis' callous attitude to collateral damage,

there's good reason to suppose that they considered the wounded pride of one of their top brass as the more significant trigger for retribution. Shortly after Britain declared war on Germany in early September 1939, Hermann Goering, head of the Luftwaffe, confidently and publicly declared:

If even a single English bomber manages to penetrate our air defences, if a single bomb should ever fall on Berlin, then I'll eat my hat.

The precise words Goering used were '. . . *dann will ich Meier heißen*' ('. . . then you can call me Meier'), a common German idiom expressing something vanishingly unlikely. The *Reichsmarschall*'s empty boast came back to haunt him, as Berlin and 130 other cities were pummelled by the RAF at night and – from late 1942 onwards – by the US Eighth Air Force by day. In private, people began referring to Hitler's designated deputy and successor as 'Herr Meier'; and even a verbal phrase – *es meiert* ('it's Meier-ing') – was coined to describe enemy air raids. Goering's excess of vanity was matched by an absence of self-deprecating wit, and such sarcasm was made punishable by death at the hands of the Gestapo. These quips formed part of a general body of highly risky jokes that did the rounds during the Third Reich (*see* Chapter 11: Laughter in the Dark). Some had as their butt the whole concept of *Vergeltung*; for instance, when the German Dad's Army '*Volkssturm*' was formed as a last-ditch measure against the invading Allies, a rhyming witticism observed: *Jetzt zieh'n sie unsern Opa ein/Das soll wohl die Vergeltung sein?* ('Now they've called up Grandpa/So that's what they call 'retribution', is it?')

The initial reaction of Londoners to the V-1s was bafflement, because the attacks did not conform to expectations. As the narrator of Graham Greene's novel, *The End of the Affair* (1951), records:

> *We had become unused to air raids. Apart from the short spell in February 1944, there had been nothing since the blitz petered out with the great final raids of 1941. When the sirens went and the first robots** came over, we assumed that a few planes had broken through our night defences. One felt a sense of grievance when the All Clear had still not sounded after an hour.*

The V-1 and V-2 were intended to sow terror among the inhabitants of London. Guidance systems were not yet sophisticated enough to direct them against military targets. Though delivering a far smaller payload, the V-1 flying bomb, a crude form of cruise missile, had the greater psychological impact. So long as you could hear its puttering motor (hence its English nickname 'doodlebug'), you were safe, but when its fuel was expended and the motor cut out, woe betide you if you were at the end of its glide path. However, the V-2 ballistic missile fell vertically from the skies at supersonic velocity, so people knew nothing of it until it hit. To quell any spread of panic about this new weapon, the British authorities tried to claim gas leaks as the cause of the first few strikes. But London's populace, ever wise and ever cynical, knew better and took to calling the V-2s 'flying gas pipes'.

*The V-weapons also included the little-known V-3, a 'supergun' installed in northern France to bombard London, but it was destroyed by RAF bombing in July 1944 before it could be used in anger.

**The use of 'robots' to describe the flying bombs wasn't an affectation of Greene's but a standard term found in newspapers, and elsewhere, in 1944. An alternative expression was 'robot bomb'. Another layer of fear was added by the complete absence of any human agency after the weapons were fired.

Chapter 10

Wartime Slogans

Etymological dictionaries reveal that 'slogan' derives from a Gaelic word from the Scottish Highlands, *sluagh-gairm*, meaning 'war cry'. Fittingly, in George Orwell's dystopian novel *Nineteen Eighty-Four* (1949), which depicts a world in a state of constant conflict, the slogan looms large. Quite literally – three huge party slogans adorn the exterior of the Ministry of Truth: WAR IS PEACE, FREEDOM IS SLAVERY, IGNORANCE IS STRENGTH. These would have struck a particular chord with Orwell's first readers; all combatant nations in World War Two, as we shall see below, browbeat their civilian populations with mottos like this. Truth is commonly said to be the first casualty of war; conversely, its first beneficiary is the sloganeer.

The Unholy Trinity

[**French:** *Travail, famille, patrie,*
'Work, family, fatherland']

The human brain seems to have a special affinity for groups of three: *Veni, vidi, vici*; Life, Liberty, and the Pursuit of Happiness; Snap, Crackle, and Pop! It is a rhetorical device known as the tricolon, or 'three-part list', and has been in the repertoire of orators since Classical antiquity.

Perhaps because they were so enamoured of classical order in general (*see* Chapter 3: The Grandeur that was Rome), totalitarian regimes of the 20th century frequently had recourse to the tricolon when exhorting their citizens to fall in line. Fascist Italy coined the slogan *Credere, obbedire, combattere* ('Believe, obey, fight'), which was emblazoned on the façades of public buildings such as barracks and assembly halls, and on factories involved in the war effort. The Third Reich had *Ein Volk, ein Reich, ein Führer* ('One People, one Empire, one Leader'), a phrase first used to appeal to a sense of shared ethnicity and statehood in the run-up to the Nazi annexation of Austria in 1938.

Yet arguably the most insidious and consistently applied of these rousing mottos was Vichy France's *Travail, famille, patrie* ('Work, family, fatherland'). This was deliberately formulated to supplant the Republican agenda of *Liberté, égalité, fraternité*; such sentiments clearly had no currency for a collaborationist régime whose stock-in-trade was deporting sections of its populace to labour, or simply to perish, in Nazi Germany. In September 1940, Vichy French leader Marshal Philippe Pétain expressly repudiated the French Republic's motto in a magazine article which concluded: 'Finally, we shall tell them [i.e. French youth] that there is no way of having true brotherhood except within those natural groups: the family, the town, the homeland.'

Travail, famille, patrie became the clarion call of the so-called *Révolution nationale*, the Pétain government's programme for the revival of the French nation after the humiliating defeat of 1940. The slogan appeared on coins minted during the Occupation, and on various propaganda posters. The best-known of these superimposed the three words on the vertical bars of the French flag, and below them the ditty:

> *Telle est aujourd'hui,*
> *Français,*
> *la tâche à laquelle*
> *je vous convie.*
> ['Today, citizen of France,
> This is the task to which I enjoin you.']

This homily was signed with a flourish: 'Ph. Pétain'. But if this personal appeal by the Saviour of Verdun should fall on deaf ears, another poster with the heading *Révolution natio-nale* drove the message home even more explicitly. On it, two houses are seen, one unstable and tumbledown – representing the Third Republic – which is shrouded in stormclouds and surmounted by a Star of David and a tattered red flag, while the other is bathed in sunlight, in spick-and-span order, and proudly flying the *tricolore*. The house in good order rests, of course, on the firm bedrock of *Travail, famille, patrie*; a quite different trinity underpins the Jewish–Bolshevik hovel: *Paresse, démagogie, internationalisme* ('Indolence, dema-goguery, internationalism').

The Popular Poster That Never Was

[British: 'Keep Calm and Carry On']

There's no getting away from it now – it's everywhere. And not just in Britain either. It's gone global, gone viral: 'Keep Calm and Carry On' has conquered the world. It, or jokey inversions of it ('Freak Out and Quit'), or obscene variations on the theme, can be seen on a wide range of household items and fashion accessories.

The irony is that the original never saw the light of day.

Created in 1939, when war was looming, it was one of a series of three posters conceived by the Ministry of Information and designed to boost the morale of a population threatened by imminent aerial bombardment. The first two proclaimed '*Your* Courage, *Your* Cheerfulness, *Your* Resolution Will Bring Us Victory' and 'Freedom Is In Peril: Defend It With All Your Might.' But in the event, the Phoney War (*see* Chapter 2: The Waiting Game) dragged on, no bombing or invasion occurred, and the public grew weary of the strident voice of officialdom. Historian Michael Balfour's book *Propaganda in War 1939–1945* (1979) explains why the campaign missed its mark:

Another cause for criticism was found in posters which had been prepared, with expert advice, in the belief that they would go up in an atmosphere of crisis caused by heavy air raids; in a wholly different context, they were greeted with disdain. One carried the words, 'Your courage, your cheerfulness, your resolution will bring us victory.' This was widely criticised as suggesting that the authorities were dissociating themselves from the ordinary man. But if the adjective had been 'our' rather than 'your', a loophole would have been provided for the individual to opt out of responsibility on the ground that other people could be relied on to cope. A more perceptive criticism was that, to many of the public, 'resolution' only meant something one made at the New Year!

The mood of popular disaffection filtered through to the men at the ministry and, despite having printed two and a half million copies of the final, famous poster, they decided against further antagonising the public and refrained from distributing them.

'Keep Calm and Carry On' resurfaced only in 2000, when the owner of Barter Books in Alnwick, Northumberland found an original poster in the bottom of a box of old books he had purchased. After he'd framed it and hung it in his shop, so many customers asked if they could buy it that he had a batch of 500 reproductions run off. The rest is history. The message it conveys is held up as an example of the best of the British phlegmatic spirit when faced with adversity: Do your worst, Mr Hitler . . . Blighty can take it! But in actual fact, the real story behind the poster reveals an equally admirable trait in the national character: an ingrained aversion to being told what to do by bumptious bureaucrats. A resounding 'Rule Britannia!' to that.

Fighting Talk

[Italian: *Boia chi Molla!*,
'Anyone who surrenders is an executioner!']

An Italian slogan indelibly associated with Fascism is the motto *Boia chi molla!* (literally: 'He who surrenders is an executioner/hangman'); the sense of it is that if you abandon the fight and cut and run, you're condemning your braver comrades to death.

The origin of the phrase has been variously traced to the French Revolution-inspired Parthenopean Republic, which broke away from the Kingdom of Naples in 1799, or the popular uprising in Milan (the so-called 'Five Days of Milan'/*Cinque giornate di Milano*) during the Year of Revolutions in 1848. Yet whatever its historical provenance, it became most famous as the battle cry of the *Arditi* (the élite Italian storm troopers who went on to form the nucleus of Mussolini's blackshirts) in World War One.

The motto was eagerly taken up by the Italian fascist movement and state. Not that it did much good in exhorting Mussolini's ill-equipped and demoralised conscripts to stand their ground in World War Two: the Italian army was humiliated in its attempted invasion of Greece in late 1940, while early the following year 115,000 Italian troops surrendered to numerically far inferior Allied forces in Operation Compass in Cyrenaica, North Africa. Remember the old schoolboy joke? Q: Which are the world's shortest books? A: The Scottish Book of Gifts, The Italian Book of War Heroes . . .

Postwar, during the civil unrest that overtook the southern region of Reggio di Calabria from July 1970 to February 1971, *Boia chi molla!* became the rallying cry of its leader Francesco Franco, a trade unionist with links to the neofascist MSI party. More recently, it has appeared as a banner flown by far-right football fans – so-called 'Ultras' – supporting clubs with traditional fascist associations, such as the Roman team S.S. (not what you're thinking; it stands for *Società Sportiva*) Lazio. Nor is it confined to the thugs on the terraces: in 1999, during his spell with FC Parma, the long-serving Italian national goalkeeper, Gianluigi Buffon, once sported a t-shirt bearing the slogan. Buffon is one of several recent or current Azzurri to harbour extreme right-wing sympathies (Paolo di Canio and Alberto Aquilani are others), and notoriously also wore on his jersey the number '88', well known as the numerical cipher for HH = 'Heil Hitler'. When taken to task, Buffon maintained that the numbers actually symbolised testicles – which, he claimed, 'you need in order to play football'. All of which was, indeed, a load of balls, though not in the sense that Buffon intended.

Bad Blood

[German: *Blut und Boden*, 'Blood and Soil']

In a famous and much-loved episode of the TV series *Hancock's Half Hour* called 'The Blood Donor' (1961) our eponymous antihero, the epitome of the bumptious Little Englander, tells a nurse who has enquired after his nationality:

Ah, you've got nothing to worry about there. It's the blood you're thinking about, isn't it? British – British, undiluted for 12 generations. One-hundred per cent Anglo-Saxon, perhaps just a dash of Viking . . . nothing else has crept in . . . It's like motor oil – it doesn't mix, if you get my meaning.

And when she patiently explains that blood transfusion has nothing to do with family background, he replies indignantly: '*I didn't come here for a lecture on Communism!*'

Appropriately enough for an ideology that has been responsible for spilling so much of it down the ages, nationalism has always been obsessed with blood. Mystical properties are ascribed to it, indelibly defining a person's race, kinship and worldview. All arrant nonsense, of course, but the idea has proved to have mileage among the gullible in straitened economic times.

Nazism generated a whole slew of terms to do with blood. These included: *Blutsvergiftung* ('blood-poisoning'; not septicaemia, but the commingling of a people's blood with that of other races, supposedly bringing about its demise); *Blutschutzgesetz* ('blood protection law'; part of the Nuremberg Laws aimed at segregating and marginalising the Jewish population, it prohibited marriage between Germans and Jews); and *Blutschande* ('blood shame'; originally 'incest', but redefined by the Nazis as sexual intercourse between a German and a person of another race). But the most pervasive and notorious use of the word 'blood' with these racial connotations was in the compound *Blut und Boden* ('Blood and Soil').

The term was first used in the late 19th century by German writers whose works espoused a kind of agrarian romanticism. Its central tenet was the intimate, unbreakable bond between the peasantry and the land they had tilled for generations. Ostensibly, this wasn't so very far removed from Thomas Hardy's contemporaneous 'novels of character and environment'. However, a nationalistic and racial undercurrent utterly alien to the Wessex writer coloured these early uses of the German phrase. Instead, the true progenitor of *Blut und Boden* was the Frenchman Maurice Barrès (1862–1923), a novelist and journalist who was a leading proponent of the theory of 'ethnic nationalism'. Barrès – a rabid Jew-hater and anti-Dreyfusard – saw the French nation as a product of the innate connection between its peasantry and the soil. The troubled history of his native region of Lorraine, on the German border, prompted him to develop a somewhat morbid concept which he called '*la terre et les morts*':

Our earth gives us discipline and we are the continuation of our dead . . . The soil speaks to us and collaborates with our national conscience.

As part of the agenda of National Socialism, *Blut und Boden* was the creation of the ideologist Richard Walther Darré, whom Hitler appointed as Minister of Food and Agriculture on his accession to power in 1933. Three years earlier, Darré had published the work *Neuadel aus Blut und Boden* ('*A New Aristocracy Based on Blood and Soil*'). This book praised the German peasant as the backbone of the nation, decrying urban culture as degenerate and cosmopolitan (and inherently Jewish, naturally) and advocating a programme of eugenics to breed a future race of strong, horny-handed Nordic sons of toil. Of course, the vision of an agrarian Utopia sat ill with Nazism's heavy reliance upon capital and industry to bankroll and build its war machine; nor, it appeared, did this noble tradition of 'blood and soil' extend to the Slavic peoples overrun and uprooted by Hitler's forces in his seizure of *Lebensraum* for the German people.

For all its patent intellectual bankruptcy, the notion of ethnic identity vouchsafed by generations of the dead and the soil in which they decompose continues to enthrall ultra-conservatives. In his 2007 polemic *State of Emergency*, the American right-wing pundit Pat Buchanan claimed that the founding fathers of the United States had a belief in 'shared ties of blood, soil, and memory'. One is left to speculate what kind of memories of blood and soil the slaves who toiled and died on those founding fathers' plantations had.

A Political Purgative

[Italian: *Olio di ricino e manganello*, 'Castor Oil and the Bludgeon']

In a speech delivered to Italy's Chamber of Deputies on

3 January 1925, Benito Mussolini gave a bravura oratorical performance, proclaiming the achievements of Fascism. At one point, to fervent applause from his supporters, he announced:

If Fascism has been nothing more than castor oil and the bludgeon [olio di ricino e manganello], and not instead a proud passion of the best of Italian youth, then the fault is all mine!

What on earth was the *Duce* talking about? The bludgeon is plain enough; like the *Sturmabteilung* (SA) in Germany, Mussolini's *Squadristi* were street-fighting thugs, notorious for meting out severe public beatings to their adversaries. But the castor oil opens up a window into a less well-known and decidedly unsalubrious piece of Italian political history. To chasten a captured foe, the Blackshirt gangs would often force-feed him a litre or so of castor oil; the debilitating bout of diarrhoea this induced was deemed a strong deterrent against further anti-Fascist agitation.* Sometimes the victim would die, especially if the oil was mixed with gasoline or if the diarrhoea caused severe dehydration, but more often the result of this enforced extreme evacuation was pain and humiliation. Like so much else in Italian Fascist ritual and practice, the castor-oil treatment is thought to have been pioneered by Gabriele D'Annunzio during his short-lived dictatorship over Fiume in 1919.

Mussolini's opponents were to repay this humiliation in spades. After the *Duce* and his mistress Clara Petacci had been captured and shot dead by partisans in April 1945, their corpses were exposed to public ridicule by being hung upside-down from meathooks beneath the canopy of a petrol-station forecourt in Milan. The circus of vengeance did not end even after his body had been cut down and taken to the local morgue. In his work *Il Duce and His Women: Mussolini's Rise to Power* (2011), historian Roberto Olla relates that hundreds of spectators filed in to view the former dictator. But not to pay their respects. 'Everyone,' Olla notes, 'wanted to take photographs of Mussolini's penis.'

*The castor-oil motif crops up in both Bernardo Bertolucci's film *The Conformist* (1970) and Federico Fellini's *Amarcord* (1973).

Chapter 11

The Home Front

In 1957, Peter Fleming – brother of Ian, the creator of James Bond – published a highly readable and well-researched account of the planned German invasion and Britain's countermeasures entitled *Invasion, 1940*. Fleming pointed out that even before the war was properly underway, as far as the British were concerned, there had already been loss: *'The loss might be expressed in terms of bereavement or of separation: of a career interrupted, a house requisitioned, a scholarship forgone: of an oak-grove felled, a flower-bed incorporated in the foundations of a pill-box, a trawler converted into a minesweeper: of anything from tragedy to inconvenience.'* His words are a reminder that, whatever the defeats and victories on the battlefield, there were innumerable consequences at home, down to the smallest detail of behaviour, and very often a price to be paid.

Dial 'A' for Aryan

[German: *Sprachreinigung*, 'language purification']

So thoroughgoing were the Nazis in their racism that they even applied ethnic cleansing to the German language. This policy brought the purging of many foreign loanwords (*das Automobil*, for instance, was replaced by the Germanised *der Kraftwagen* ['powered carriage'] and *das Telefon* – in use since its invention – by *der Fernsprecher*, literally 'far-speaker'). Indeed, it is from the seemingly innocuous realm of telephony, specifically the telephonic alphabet, that the depth of their mania emerges.

By 1903, the German Postal Service, which was responsible for the phone system, had come up with a set of mnemonic names for the individual letters of the alphabet. This meant that users, when trying to place a call with an operator down a crackly, voice-distorting line, could clearly enunciate the name of the person they wished to be connected to. So, the name 'Maier' became '**M**arie **A**nton **I**sidor **E**mil **R**ichard'. Some of the names chosen were Biblical in origin, like 'Samuel,' 'David' and 'Zacharias'. For the next three decades, this arrangement remained largely unaltered. Then, on 22 March 1933, the Postal Administration in Rostock received the following communication from a nationalistically-minded local telephone subscriber, one Johannes Schliemann:

> *Sirs,*
> *In view of the great change the German nation has undergone, I no longer think it appropriate to retain Jewish names such as David, Nathan, Samuel, etc. in the spelling table in the telephone book. I presume that suitable German names can be found. I trust that my suggestion will be taken up in the next edition of the book.*

Despite some initial resistance from the bureaucrats, soon enough a biddable zealot implemented Herr Schliemann's suggestion, and Dora, Nordpol (= 'North Pole'), Siegfried (note the Wagnerian touch) and Zeppelin duly replaced the offending

Semitic-sounding names. The new spelling alphabet was also used in radio communication, for the call signs of aircraft. The practice even spread beyond the realm of communications: successive variants of Willy Messerschmitt's famous Bf109 fighter plane – the 109E, F and G – were known respectively as the 'Emil', 'Fritz' and 'Gustav'.

The German telephonic alphabet was officially 'de-Nazified' in 1948, and most of the original names were reinstated. Most, but not all: the ideologically untainted 1933 entries Dora and Nordpol still remain.

Victor Klemperer (1881–1960), cousin of the composer and conductor Otto Klemperer and an academic of Jewish origin who converted to Protestantism in 1912, wrote a fascinating postwar account of the Nazis' use and perversion of language, entitled *LTI – Lingua Tertii Imperii; Notizbuch eines Philologen* ('*Language of the Third Reich: a philologist's notebook*' (1947)). In it, Klemperer recounts how all references to Jewish scientists were proscribed at the Technical University of Dresden where he was Professor of Romance Philology, a post from which he was summarily dismissed in 1935:

In the Physics Department, the name Einstein had to be hushed up, and the 'Hertz' unit of frequency could also not be referred to by its Jewish name.

Cooper's Snoopers and the Nun with the Stubble

[British: Fifth Column]

The expression 'fifth column' emerged out of the Spanish Civil War. Soon after that conflict started in 1936 a rebel general was asked by a reporter which of four converging columns of troops would capture Madrid, one of the cities in the hands of the Republican (i.e. anti-Fascist) forces. The reply, that Madrid would fall to a 'fifth column' (in Spanish, *una quinta columna*), implied that there were enough sympathisers inside the city to rise up and assist when the assault came from outside. The expression quickly caught on. Ernest Hemingway, acting as a war correspondent and with Republican loyalties, took it as the title for his only play, staged in 1937 in Madrid while the city was still under siege.

Fears about Nazi spies and would-be collaborators made 'fifth column' a natural phrase for Winston Churchill to employ in the early stages of World War Two, when alarm about an invasion of Britain was at its height. The term was in everyday use. As Mr Grant from the 'Ministry of Requirements' explains to Agatha Christie's sleuthing duo, Tommy and Tuppence Beresford, in the spy thriller *N or M?* (1941):

Our danger is the danger of Troy – the wooden horse within our walls. Call it the Fifth Column if you like. It is here, among us. Men and women, some of them highly placed, some of them obscure, but all believing genuinely in the Nazi aims and the Nazi creed and desiring to substitute that sternly efficient creed for the muddled easy-going liberty of our democratic institutions.*

Belief in the existence of a Fifth Column was reinforced by German propaganda broadcasts in English, particularly those put out by the NBBS (New British Broadcasting Station). These transmissions, which ended with the National Anthem and were purportedly made from England itself, were spoken in the tones of a true 'patriot' and stressed how everyone hated the British leaders and had a longing for peace.

To oppose the machinations of the Fifth Columnists, a nebulous, self-appointing group called the Silent Column was created by Duff Cooper, the Minister of Information. Through posters and cinema advertising, the public was encouraged to point the finger of shame at figures with cartoonish names like 'Miss Leaky Mouth' and 'Mr Glumpot'; in other words those who disparaged Britain's chances in the conflict. Offenders against official optimism could be taken to court. The campaign backfired badly. Encouraging people to snoop on their neighbours or even to denounce them was un-British, if not actually reminiscent of Nazi behaviour. 'Cooper's Snoopers', as they were known, soon dwindled away.

The justified fear of airborne attacks and suspicion about the existence of traitors overlapped. There were innumerable reports to the police, Home Guard and other authorities of sinister flashes of light coming from ground level during air raids, even though the idea that anyone could direct the Luftwaffe by fiddling about with a torch in his back garden was, objectively, ridiculous. Similarly, there was a fear of spies and saboteurs descending through the air to be assisted by sympathisers on the ground. 'Parachutes and Traitors: More Suggestions' was the heading on a letters column in *The Times* in May 1940. How to spot the parachutist, if he was devious enough to be in disguise, became a preoccupation.

From Holland came the legend that German paratroopers had arrived there dressed as nuns. This was too good to be true but the idea gripped people right across the social spectrum: a *Daily Express* cartoon showed a stubbly nun in army boots, sitting at a bar and saying 'Of course at the moment it's just a suspicion,' while novelist Virginia Woolf whispered to her husband Leonard as a nun got into their train carriage that this was really 'a Nazi paratrooper in disguise'. The possibility of such disguised infiltration meant that the BBC warned German listeners that any parachutist descending in anything 'other than recognised German uniform' would be shot straightaway.

As the threat of invasion faded and Hitler's Operation Sea Lion (*Seelöwe*), the German code name for the invasion, was indefinitely postponed, the paranoia about spies and fifth columnists also abated. It reached its natural peak in the early stages of the war, as can be seen in films such as *Went the Day Well?* (*see* Chapter 3: English Pastoral). It also emerges in popular thrillers like Christie's *N or M?* or Hammond Innes's *Wreckers Must Breathe* (1940) in which an entire U-boat base with seven submarine pens is covertly constructed in caves on the Cornish coast, and in literary fiction such as Elizabeth Bowen's *The Heat of the Day* (1949) set during the Blitz and turning on the possibility that the lover of the central female character might be a spy.

*Incidentally, it was Christie's use of the name Bletchley for a retired major in her thriller *N or M?* that caused MI5 to take an interest in her. Since the code-breaking work at Bletchley Park was the most secret British activity of the war, the appearance of the name in a spy novel, together with the author's friendship with one of the principal code breakers (himself bound by the Official Secrets Act), caused ripples of concern. Luckily, and in reply to some casual questioning, Christie explained that she'd given the tedious major the name of Bletchley because she had been stuck there on the train between Oxford and London. It was a little act of revenge.

A Medieval Throwback

[German: *Gau/Gauleiter*, **Nazi administrative division; regional governor]**

The noun *der Gau* originally denoted a tract of land settled by a Germanic tribe. In the Frankish Empire and throughout the Middle Ages, the term broadly approximated to the English 'shire', but by the late 18th century it had fallen into disuse; a dictionary of the period described it as 'largely obsolete'. Nowadays, it only lives on in certain historical place names, e.g. Breisgau, the area around Freiburg in south-west Germany, or Allgäu, a region in the far south of Bavaria.

In the early- to mid-19th century, as nationalist movements sought to weld the various kingdoms, petty principalities and bishoprics that made up German-speaking Central Europe into a single polity, the *Gau* was mooted as the main subdivision of the new state. The German-Jewish radical and satirist Ludwig Börne (1786–1837) lampooned these aspirations:

Now I see through the whole farce. Ghost tales from the Middle Ages . . . If they'd talked in terms of provinces, I'd have simply told them they were godforsaken reprobates. But their mention of Gaus only leads me to say: 'You're nothing but buffoons hankering after "ye-olde-Germanie!"'

Given its Teutonic heritage and nationalistic pedigree, the Nazis were keen to adopt the *Gau* as the highest administrative division of the Reich. Thirty-three of them were established in Germany; as other areas of Europe fell to conquest, *Gaus* were also set up there, under the control of

143

local fifth-columnists who had shown themselves sympathetic to the National Socialist cause. For instance, Konrad Henlein, head of the right-wing ethnic German party in the Sudetenland area of Czechoslovakia, was made *Gauleiter* there when it was annexed in 1938. Likewise, the Belgian Rexist Léon Degrelle was rewarded for betraying his country and for his service in the Waffen-SS by being placed in charge of Wallonia. One of the most notorious of these regional governors was the Austrian Odilo Globocnik, *Gauleiter* of Vienna from 1938–9; dismissed for illegal foreign currency speculation, he went on to become a key figure in Operation Reinhard (*see* Chapter 14: Glossing over Genocide), the transportation and murder of two million Polish Jews and Roma. Robert Harris made Globocnik the sadistic arch-villain of his alternate historical novel *Fatherland*.

One of the stranger stories from World War Two concerns the occult thriller writer Dennis Wheatley. Soon after war broke out, he was telephoned by a friend in the security services, who asked him if he knew a William Joyce. Wheatley was at a loss to recall anyone of that name but later, while chatting to his wife about the phone call, was reminded by her that a man named Joyce had attended one of their house parties in St John's Wood six months previously. This small, scar-faced man had engaged the novelist in conversation about Germany (Wheatley had lived there for a spell after World War One) and confided in him that Hermann Goering was a great fan of his work. When Wheatley called his spy friend back to give him this information, the latter revealed that Joyce (later to gain notoriety as the propaganda broadcaster 'Lord Haw-Haw'; *see* Chapter 13 'Germany Calling') was a Nazi agitator who had long been under surveillance but had escaped the dragnet when war was declared. Then, in an almost offhand way, he announced: 'We got all his papers and his card indexes, and in them you're noted to be proposed as "*Gauleiter* for north London".'

Lost in Translation

[French: *se faire appeler Arthur,*
'to get yourself called Arthur']

A little linguistic curio emerges from the four-year occupation of France (1940–44) by the German Army in the form of an idiomatic – and still current – phrase meaning 'to be given a dressing-down': *se faire appeler Arthur* (literally 'to get yourself called Arthur').

This term supposedly originated in the curfew that was imposed across northern France by the military authorities. People in danger of not making it home before the curfew deadline of 20.00 hours would be sharply reprimanded by German patrols with a shout of '*Acht Uhr!*' ('Eight o'clock!'). This guttural utterance was misheard by the French and corrupted into 'Arthur'.

Some scholars dispute this etymology, however, claiming an earlier origin for the idiom. Certainly, the neat story above is suspect as regards timing: various sources place the curfew start time throughout the *zone occupée* at either 22.00 or 23.00 but none as early as eight in the evening. But even if we are dealing here with what anthropologists call an 'aetiological myth' – a tale concocted *post hoc* to explain the provenance of names or phenomena – it's nice to think of the French pinning a phrase concerning harsh reproach on their overbearing neighbours to the east.

One time-related issue beyond doubt is that all clocks in the occupied zone were moved forward one hour to accord with the Central European Time used in Germany (up to the war, France had been on Greenwich Mean Time). Despite the repudiation of everything else to do with the hated occupation, CET was retained post-1945 and remains in force in France to this day.

Lines of Defence
[British: Pillboxes]

In the 18th century a pillbox was a box for holding pills; in the 19th century it described a style of hat; and by the 20th century the pillbox had grown to become a ubiquitous part of Britain's defences against a potential Nazi invasion. It was the German army who first built pillboxes – small, circular concrete fortifications used as gun emplacements – in the closing stages of World War One. The threat of Operation Sea Lion (*Seelöwe*), the German code name for the invasion that never happened, prompted the eventual construction of some 28,000 pillboxes around Britain. To counter any German tank advance, dozens of defensive 'stop lines' were constructed across the country, consisting of ditches, concrete blocks (sometimes known as 'dragon's teeth') and pillboxes. The principal one, the GHQ – General Headquarters – Line, ran from the Bristol Channel to the Thames Estuary before curving northwards as far as Yorkshire.

Local builders constructed the pillboxes to Ministry of Defence specifications. Typically, a thin shell of brick was reinforced with concrete and steel while refinements included internal walls to guard against ricochets and asbestos flaps in case the Germans tried flamethrowers against the occupants.

The most distinguished pillbox must be Fort Henry near Poole in Dorset. In April 1944, from this ugly concrete construction perched above the beach and overlooking Studland Bay, King George VI, Winston Churchill, General Eisenhower and General Montgomery watched a dress rehearsal exercise for the D-Day invasion which was to take place two months later.

Around a quarter of the pillboxes still survive, a handful of them listed by English Heritage. There is also a society dedicated to studying and preserving them (www.pillbox-study-group.org.uk). Any rambler across the English countryside, and in suburban areas too, is likely to have seen one of these relics of the war, overgrown and dilapidated but stolidly evocative of a different age.

Springtime for Hitler

[**German:** *Führerwetter*, 'Leader's weather']

In Britain, anyone trying to hitch their political fortunes to the weather or pit their authority against the forces of nature would be on a decidedly sticky wicket. Millennia of meteorological capriciousness have disabused us of any such foolishness. English rulers have known this ever since King Canute sat on the Southampton foreshore and showed his fawning acolytes that his temporal power could not stem the tide (an apocryphal story, but the point still stands).

Not so in Germany, at least from the late-19th century onward. The more settled nature of the continental climate, which saw a string of Emperor Wilhelm II's official engagements blessed with fine weather, led some royalist commentators to coin the term *Kaiserwetter* – 'Emperor's weather' – the implication being that even the heavens smiled down on their august ruler. The phrase stuck and passed into popular parlance. Predictably, when Hitler came to power (and, again, various NSDAP rallies and other celebrations such as Hitler's spring birthday – 20 April – basked in fair conditions), the Nazis co-opted the term, calling it either *Führerwetter* or *Hitlerwetter*. Its first usage is not recorded, but it was certainly a well-known phenomenon, even beyond Germany's borders, by the outbreak of war. On 2 October 1939, for instance, *Time* magazine reported:

> *Amid the brilliant sunshine which Germans call 'Hitler weather'– they used to call it 'Kaiser weather' – the Führer rumbled off to Danzig in a six-wheeled juggernaut staff car, followed by two Gestapo cars in which guards sat fingering new-style German repeater rifles.*

Soon enough, though, an icy gloom was to darken this rosy picture. In late 1941, as he had done a century and more before against Napoleon, Russia's 'General Winter' entered the fray, freezing even the fuel in the Wehrmacht's lorries and tanks, giving poorly-clad German troops frostbite and causing Operation Barbarossa to grind to a crawl. When the spring thaw came, the ensuing quagmire was even worse. Not much talk of *Führerwetter* then.

Big Brother is Watching You

[Italian: *Testa di Morto*, 'Death's Head']

Surprisingly, Benito Mussolini seems to have had few nicknames. You might imagine that this gurning, bull-necked blowhard would have attracted a swarm of disparaging soubriquets, but no. It may simply be that Italians prefer their politicians to behave like characters from *opera buffa*: how else are we to account for Silvio Berlusconi's popular appeal?

Mussolini did have one intriguing name, though, which derived from a public sculpture of him. Artistic representations of the *Duce* were thick on the ground in 1930s Italy; futurism in particular, the Italian strain of modernism and a cultural fellow-traveller of Fascism, was fond of portraying him. A famous 360-degree bust ('Continuous Profile'; 1933) by the sculptor Renato Giuseppe Bertelli (now in the collection of the Imperial War Museum) was meant to make Mussolini appear the epitome of streamlined modernity and dynamism. In truth, it only succeeds in making him look like a ceramic electricity power-line insulator.

The Palazzo Braschi in Rome, which during the 21 years of the dictatorship served as the National Fascist Party headquarters, housed a far more naturalistic depiction of the leader. This took the form of a huge stone face of *Il Duce* leering down from on high; behind it, the entire façade of the building was covered with a placard proclaiming, 132 times over: 'SI, SI, SI, SI . . .' ('YES, YES, YES, YES . . .'), an orgasmic affirmation of Italy's infatuation with her political strongman. Unfortunately, Mussolini's massive mug looked like nothing so much as an outsized death mask, and so opponents took to calling him *Testa di Morto* ('Death's Head'). As with Italian Fascism as a whole, it's hard to say which aspect of this macabre tableau predominates – the sinister or the risible.

Historic Destruction
[British: **The Baedeker raids**]

The travel guides published by the Prussian-born Karl Baedeker from the 1830s soon won acclaim for their detail and reliability. In 1846, Baedeker introduced his star system for the 'must-visit' places, and long before the 20th century the mere word 'Baedeker' became synonymous with 'guidebook'. When the RAF bombed the historic ports of Lübeck and Rostock, the Luftwaffe launched retaliatory raids on the English cities of Bath, Canterbury, Exeter, Norwich and York. These targets seem to have been chosen for their cultural, rather than strategic, importance and the story goes that a German foreign ministry spokesman declared that the Luftwaffe would bomb every English building marked with three stars in Baedeker's guide. Doubt has been cast on the accuracy of this account, not least because Baedeker employed only a one- or two-star system. The Baedeker raids, sometimes known as the Baedeker Blitz, lasted from April to June 1942, leaving over 3,000 civilians killed or wounded. When in the following year the British bombed Leipzig, the Baedeker publishing house was completely destroyed by fire. The name and the reputation survived, however, and the brand was relaunched in Germany in 2005.

Laughter in the Dark
[German: *Flüsterwitze*, 'whispered jokes']

There's nothing like a joke, verbal or visual, for puncturing the pomposity of power. Politicians tend not to like ones at their expense; John Major famously hated *Guardian* cartoonist Steve Bell's portrayal of him wearing his Y-fronts outside his trousers, an image of comic ineptitude that dogged him throughout his time in his office.

Totalitarian states are even pricklier about mickey-takers. When your whole political philosophy is predicated on blind obedience, you can't afford to have waspish satirists on the sidelines mocking your every mistake and foible.* Jokesmiths in the Third Reich were soon to learn quite how intolerant the Nazis were: in 1934, just a year after Hitler took power, a new law enacted severe penalties against anyone who dared to speak up, humorously or otherwise, against the regime. The *Heimtückegesetz zur Bekämpfung von Verleumdungen des Regimes* ('Malice Law against Casting Aspersions on the Regime') imposed custodial sentences on those found guilty of undermining the German people's morale – so-called *Volksschädlinge* ('antisocial parasites').

Even in such draconian circumstances, though, the human spirit proved unquenchable. Under the menacing shadow of a visit from the Gestapo, a body of witticisms emerged, growing larger as the defeats mounted and privations at home multiplied. They were known collectively and for obvious reasons as *Flüsterwitze* ('whispered jokes'). Here are just a few of them:

Q: Hitler, Goering and Goebbels are sitting in an air-raid shelter. Who will be saved if the shelter receives a direct hit?

A: Germany.

Following his capture, Rudolf Hess [Hitler's second-in-command who flew to Britain in 1941 to try and negotiate peace] is introduced to Churchill, who asked him: 'So, you're the madman, eh?' Hess replies: 'No, I'm just his deputy!'

Q: Who are the three greatest photographers in the world?
A: Mussolini, Hitler and Goebbels: Mussolini develops, Hitler copies and Goebbels enlarges.

Goebbels starts to think that Hitler has got too big for his boots. So one day he goes to him and suggests that 'Heil Hitler!' should be replaced by the old German greeting 'Good day!'.

'No, no, my dear Goebbels,' Hitler replies, 'there'll be no good days while I'm still in power!'

Q: What's the difference between Christianity and National Socialism?
A: In Christianity, one man died for all of us. In National Socialism, we're all supposed to die for one man.

A Nazi storm trooper whispers to his mate: 'The Reichstag's on fire!'
'Shh!' answers his friend, putting his finger to his lips and glancing round nervously, 'that's only supposed to happen tomorrow!'

*As testament to the power of the satirical pen, New Zealand-born cartoonist David Low, whose drawings in the *Evening Standard* regularly skewered the Nazi leadership, was included in the Gestapo's so-called 'Black Book', the list of those to be detained in Britain after a successful German invasion (see p. 22).

Digging In
[British/German: 'Paddock'/*Adlerhorst*, 'Eagle's Eyrie'/*Wolfsschanze*, 'Wolf's Lair']

The War Cabinet remained in London during the conflict but a last redoubt was constructed in secret on the outskirts of the capital, to be used if the Battle of Britain were lost. The code name for the underground command centre was 'Paddock'. In his memoirs, Churchill claimed it was near Hampstead, but in fact Paddock was in Neasden, the north-west London suburb which has long been the butt of jokes in the satirical magazine *Private Eye*. Neasden was chosen because it was the site of a secret Post Office research centre. The Paddock bunker was used for a cabinet meeting only once in a dress rehearsal for events which, fortunately, never materialised.

The combination of Paddock and Neasden is about as far away as one can get from the Wagnerian sonorousness of Hitler's hideouts, of which the most famous were the *Adlerhorst* ('Eagle's Eyrie') in the Taunus Mountains and the *Wolfsschanze* (literally 'Wolf's Redoubt', but usually referred to in English as the 'Wolf's Lair') in East Prussia. It was from the latter that Hitler oversaw the invasion of the Soviet Union and where he also narrowly escaped assassination at the hands of Count von Stauffenberg in July 1944. Adolf Hitler was partial to Wolf-terminology; it was the pseudonym he'd used in his early political, rabble-rousing days when he wanted to avoid recognition. Other military headquarters used by the dictator were similarly titled (e.g. *Wolfsschlucht* I and II – 'Wolf's Gorge' – in Belgium and occupied France respectively).

Strutting Coxcombs

[German: *Goldfasane*, 'golden pheasants']

British fiction writers who have made the Third Reich their subject have done their research well. In two highly praised counterfactual novels, where Hitler's Germany has emerged triumphant, Robert Harris's *Fatherland* (1992) and C.J.

Sansom's *Dominion* (2012), Nazi party officials are referred to as 'golden pheasants'. The crime writer Philip Kerr, meanwhile, gave this a wry twist in imagining his central character, the hard-boiled Berlin gumshoe Bernie Gunther, as the originator of the term:

> *Their light brown tunics and red armbands made them easy to spot, which makes me think that Nazi officials and pheasants had something in common. You didn't have to know anything about them personally to want to shoot one.*
>
> *(If the Dead Rise Not, 2009)*

Harris, Kerr and Sansom were spot-on: in Hitler's Germany high-ranking Nazi Party functionaries were indeed known in popular parlance as *Goldfasane* – an allusion to their light-brown uniforms and tan leather boots and belts, adorned with copious gold braid and the red of party badges and swastika armbands. The fact that pheasants are strutting fowl, more decorative than useful, only sharpened the joke. Public resentment focused on the charmed life of privilege enjoyed by these apparatchiks while the rest of the nation made sacrifices; the perception of nepotism was widespread: one quip reworked the Nazi Party acronym NSDAP as N*a, suchst Du auch ein Pöstchen?* ('So, you're after a little sinecure too, are you?')

Pheasant-in-chief Hermann Goering, a vainglorious man whose wardrobe went unmatched until Liberace, was the target of especial vitriol: alongside his 'Herr Meier' nickname (*see* Chapter 9: Herr Meier's Empty Boast), the Reichsmarschall's fondness for martial bling earned him the title of *Lametta-Heini* ('Tinsel-Twerp').

Chapter 12

Enemy Aliens

The defeat of the Axis forces in 1945 was absolute, 'unconditional surrender' having been a part of Allied policy since President Roosevelt announced it – to Churchill's surprise – at the Casablanca Conference in January 1943. But there was one small victory which some of the defeated nations obtained: the adoption by the victors of various 'enemy' words and phrases and their assimilation into English.

Imperial Sacrifice

[**Japanese:** *Kamikaze/Banzai*]

Inevitably, Germany was responsible for the majority of foreign expressions which found a home in English, whether new ones such as flak (an abbreviation of *Fliegerabwehrkanone*, 'pilot defence gun'), Blitz or Gestapo, or older terms like *ersatz* (from the German for 'compensation' or 'replacement') which acquired resonance at a time when people had to make do with substitute or inferior goods. But other enemy nations also did their bit in enriching the language. Japan provided *kamikaze* to describe both the pilots and the planes which launched suicidal attacks on Allied shipping in the Pacific, particularly large targets like aircraft carriers and landing craft. Literally, *kamikaze* means 'divine wind', and referred to the storms which destroyed two Mongol invasion fleets sent against Japan by Kublai Khan in 1274 and 1281. An estimated 5,000 kamikaze pilots died between October 1944 and August 1945, some of them in mass sorties poetically termed *kikusui* ('floating chrysanthemums').* A similar sense of heroic self-destruction could be evoked by the war cry *Banzai*, literally meaning 'ten thousand years' and originally a greeting to the Japanese Emperor. The expression was occasionally used in the US to characterise a reckless enemy attack as well as being a familiar speech-bubble to readers of the gung-ho *Commando* comic books published in the UK from the early 1960s. Incidentally, *gung-ho* was a Chinese term picked up by the commander of the US Marines in 1942. Deriving from two words, *kung* and *ho* (work + together), 'gung-ho' swiftly became exotic shorthand for 'zealous cooperation'.

*The floral theme was continued with a purpose-built rocket-powered kamikaze flying bomb called the *Ohka* ('cherry blossom') developed late in the war. American sailors took to calling it the *Baka* bomb (*Baka* is Japanese for 'idiot' or 'fool') instead.

Symbol of Authority

[**Italian:** *Fasci di Combattimento*]

Italy's most potent linguistic contribution to the warlike atmosphere which predominated in the 1930s were the terms 'fascist' and 'fascism'. These came to characterise not only Mussolini's rule over Italy but also the ethos of Hitler's Germany as well as lesser dictatorships like Franco's in Spain or Salazar's in Portugal. Although there is much debate about various elements which contributed to fascism (doctrinal, nationalistic, racialist, anti-Semitic, etc.) there is no doubt about the historical roots of the term. As discussed previously, in ancient Rome, *fasces* was the Latin term for a bundle of rods wrapped round an axe and carried by the attendants of the magistrates (the lictors) as a symbol of their masters' authority. In 19th-century Italian, *fasci*, the plural form of *fascio* (bundle), took on the sense of 'league' or 'union', but with distinct political overtones. Mussolini appropriated the term when he formed the paramilitary *Fasci di Combattimento* (League of Combat) in 1919 which soon became the *Partito Nazionale Fascista* (National Fascist Party) and, under that name, gained power in 1922. The symbolism of the bundle of rods containing the axe remained highly significant in its representation of not only naked power but also strength through unity, since a bundle of sticks is much harder to break than a single one. In addition, a large part of Mussolini's effort was an attempt to recall, even to resurrect, the imperium of ancient Rome, even if he got no further than aping its trappings.

Bywords for Treachery
[Norwegian/French: quisling/Pétainism/Vichy]

Norway bequeathed the term *quisling* to the world. Long before the German invasion of his country, Vidkun Quisling (1887–1945) founded the Norwegian Fascist National Union Party and in 1942 became 'Minister-President' under the Nazi occupation. Put on trial at the end of the war and executed by firing squad, his surname – soon spelled with a lower-case 'q' – was synonymous with treachery and collaboration from the earliest stages of the conflict.

Two eponymous words from France embodied defeatism and collaboration. Marshal Pétain was the French head of state after the armistice was declared with Germany in June 1940 and the country was in effect split into two (the *zone occupée* and the *zone libre*). In a famous humiliation, the French delegation was compelled to meet Hitler in the same railway carriage in the forest of Compiègne where the 1918 armistice, signalling Germany's original defeat, had been signed. Pétain and Pétainism not only represented collaboration but also the deeply conservative and nationalistic administration over which this 84-year-old man presided. Pétain's government installed itself in the spa town of Vichy in central France. This was meant to be a staging post before a return to Paris but, in the event, Vichy lasted until the 1944 liberation of France despite becoming increasingly compromised, even enthusiastic, in its dealings with the Nazis (*see* Chapter 14: France's Shame). Like quisling, 'Vichyite' was soon synonymous with 'collaborator', and the name became so toxic that in at least one New York restaurant the soup known as *vichyssoise* (because it had supposedly been created in Vichy) was rechristened 'de Gaullesoise' after General Charles de Gaulle, the London-based leader of the free French forces. Even Auguste Escoffier, the doyen of cookery books, declared in 1941 that *vichyssoise* was 'now called Crème Gauloise'.

Storm and Strafe

[German: *Sturmtruppen, Feldgrau, strafen*; 'storm troop(er)s', 'field-grey', 'punish (strafe)']

Interestingly, several German words associated with World War Two that became household terms in English in fact date back to the Great War or earlier. 'Storm troop(er)' is a case in point: the term was widely used by the British press to describe members of Ernst Röhm's SA or *Sturmabteilung* ('storm division'), the street-fighting thugs who attacked Jewish businesses and battled with political opponents during Hitler's rise to power. But the term was first assimilated into English in 1917 as a direct loan-translation of the German *Sturmtruppen*, the shock troops who specialised in lightning assaults on enemy trenches using the newly developed submachine guns and flamethrowers. These units played a major role in General Erich Ludendorff's initially highly successful 'Spring Offensive' of March 1918.

Likewise, 'field-grey' (*Feldgrau*), the characteristic grey-green hue of Wehrmacht uniforms, was first noted in the 1911 edition of *Encyclopedia Britannica* as the standard colour of the uniforms of the Imperial German Army. Finally, the verb 'to strafe' is so familiar in English that we do not even register its German origin; we tend to associate it with ground attacks by fighter aircraft in World War Two, swooping down and machine-gunning columns of troops or civilians. But in fact the term derives from the verb *strafen*, meaning 'to punish', and entered English public consciousness in World War One through the slogan *Gott strafe England!* ('May God punish England!), the coinage of German-Jewish poet Ernst Lissauer. The phrase was widely reproduced on posters, stamps, beer mats, items such as cufflinks and lapel badges sold to aid the war effort, and even lignite (brown coal) fire bricks. On 1 November 1916, the *Daily Mail* reported:

The word strafe is now almost universally used. Not only is an effective bombardment of the enemy's lines or a successful trench raid described by Tommy as 'strafing the Fritzes', but there are occasions when certain 'brass hats' . . . are strafed by imprecation. And quite recently the present writer heard a working-class woman . . . shout to one of her offspring 'Wait till I git 'old of yer, I'll strafe yer, I will!'

Doing Time
[German/Russian: *Stalag/Gulag*]

Prison overcrowding, a nagging problem in peacetime, may become an extreme condition during war. Prisoners-of-war are, of course, distinct from ordinary civilian prisoners, but they, too, have to be confined and cared for, even if care is a flexible concept in wartime. In Britain, for the duration of the war and afterwards, up to 400,000 prisoners were kept in more than a thousand camps right across the United Kingdom. Although numbers were low at the start, eventual British successes, especially in the North African campaign, made for sudden, almost overwhelming increases. A front-line message after the battle of El Alamein reported that, in the absence of exact figures, the prisoner tally amounted to 'about five acres of officers and two hundred acres of other ranks'. Tracing the whereabouts of the now-forgotten POW camps in the UK has become an archaeological project; a list and commentary can be downloaded from the English Heritage website (*see Prisoners of War Camps (1939–1948) Twentieth Century Military Recording Project*).

While Britain's wartime prison camps have disappeared almost entirely from sight and memory, the linguistic traces of German ones are, ironically, still with us. The Nazi handling of prisoners varied from the relatively humane to the extremely brutal, and British POWs – regarded officially as fellow Aryans by their captors – were well treated in comparison to, say, the Russians. There were three types of camps for British and other Western prisoners: *Offizierslager/Oflag* (officers' camp), *Stammlager/Stalag* (main camp, i.e. for private soldiers and NCOs) and *Durchgangslager/Dulag* (transit camp). Of these, *Stalag* still has currency not only in POW stories and films like *The Great Escape* (1963)*, but as a general term for an ugly/ repressive set-up or construction ('[It] reminded me of the development invading the green belt south of Cambridge, known to the locals as Stalag 3 but of course praised by the planners' (*Daily Telegraph*)).

In British legend, Colditz is the daddy of all the POW camps. A castle in Saxony constructed in 1014, Colditz (*Oflag IVC*) initially housed Polish and French officers but then became the camp of (German) choice for inveterate escapers from various nations. The British experience became a best-selling book by Pat Reid, *The Colditz Story* (1952), and a film of the same name as well as a long-running TV series. The Saxon castle has entered the English language as a synonym for any forbidding prison-like structure but, because of the ingenuity of the many escape attempts (including one which involved building a glider), Colditz also carries connotations of resilience and derring-do. It was most likely the prison sense of the word that Prince Charles had in mind when he referred to Gordonstoun, his Scottish boarding school, as 'Colditz in kilts'.

The Soviet Union gave the world the *Gulag*, an acronym from the first letters of the bureaucratic title (in translation), Chief Administration for Corrective Labour Camps. This was a secret police (NKVD) department dedicated to running labour camps for dissidents and political prisoners, in which privation and brutality were so universal that the average life expectancy was one winter. Although the *Gulag* system had been known about in the West since the late 1920s, it did not become generally familiar as a word until the publication of Alexander Solzhenitsyn's *The Gulag Archipelago* (1973–6). Unlike Hitler, Stalin imprisoned, principally, his own people and did so by the million but, in August 1945 at the end of the war in the Far East, hundreds of thousands of defeated Japanese soldiers were also caught up in the *Gulag* system, and many were worked to death. Like *Stalag* and Colditz, though more inappropriately, *Gulag* is often used out of context, for example, to describe old-style holiday camps in Britain.

*What everyone remembers from this highly fictionalised film account of the famous mass escape from Stalag Luft III are Steve McQueen's motorbike exploits. McQueen played Captain Virgil Hilts, the 'Cooler King', an allusion to his skill at escaping from prison (the 'cooler') but with a sideways glance at McQueen's cool reputation.

'Cooler' was and is one of several general US terms for prison, while specifically military prisons are the 'stockade' and the 'brig' (originally on a ship and so primarily a naval term). The British equivalent in World War Two was the 'glasshouse', so called from the glassed-roofed detention centre at Aldershot Barracks and later applied to any military prison.

Chapter 13

People and Places

The names of certain locations and individuals will forever be associated with World War Two. Inevitably, many of the place names commemorate military victories or defeats – Stalingrad, El Alamein, Kursk, Dunkirk or Pearl Harbor. But in a war that, for the first time, targeted civilian populations on a massive scale, other names, such as Auschwitz, Katyn, Oradour-sur-Glane, Wannsee and Dresden, have taken their place in the dismal annals of atrocity. Meanwhile, the people discussed here are mainly, though not exclusively, a rogue's gallery of intriguing misfits.

Rallying Point
[**German:** *Nürnberg/Reichsparteitage,*
Nuremberg/Nazi Party Congresses]

The city of Nuremberg in the northern Bavarian region of Franconia will forever be associated with the rise and fall of Nazism. Every September from 1933 to 1938 the city hosted the Nuremberg Rallies, mass gatherings of the party faithful that became a byword for demagogic oratory and uncritical adulation. The third such occasion, in 1935, saw the passing of the two infamous 'Nuremberg Laws', legal instruments by which the Nazi Party deprived Jews of German citizenship (the

'Reich Citizenship Statute') and outlawed intermarriage or extramarital relations between Jews and Germans (the 'Blood Protection Statute'; *see* Chapter 10: Bad Blood). Finally, in a considered act of retribution, not unlike Hitler's choice of location for the French surrender in 1940 (*see* Chapter 12: Bywords for Treachery), the victorious Allies chose Nuremberg as the site for their trials of Nazi war criminals.

How did Nuremberg become the hub of National Socialism? After all, the German city Hitler called home after leaving his native Austria, and where he began his political agitation in 1920, was Munich (the so-called 'capital city of the movement'; *see* below). But after the failure of the 'Beer Hall Putsch' in 1923, Hitler had been banned from making any public speeches in the Bavarian capital. His power base had always been in the south – like many southern Germans and Austrians to this day, he despised all things 'Prussian' (i.e. North German) and harboured a particular hatred of 'Red' Berlin – and Nuremberg became the obvious choice. First, it was steeped in the kind of historical associations the Nazis admired: in the 13th and 14th centuries, the town's Jews had been the victims of repeated pogroms and were expelled entirely in 1499. Second, it was the home town of Hans Sachs (1494–1576), cobbler, poet and confederate of the anti-Semitic Protestant Reformer Martin Luther (Sachs also appears in Richard Wagner's 1868 opera *Die Meistersinger von Nürnberg*). Finally, Nuremberg had long been the stamping-ground of two important allies, the print works owner and later mayor, Willy Liebel, and the publisher of the weekly National Socialist newspaper *Der Stürmer* (founded 1923), Julius Streicher – party members since 1925 and 1922 respectively. As was common in Hitler's intentionally divide-and-rule management of the Nazi élite, the two men loathed one another; notwithstanding this feud, the thoroughly sympathetic attitude of the city's administration and police force made it an ideal place to locate the Party Congresses (*Reichsparteitage*). Each of these mass rallies, held on a specially constructed parade ground to the southeast of the city centre and attended by around 700,000 supporters, had its own title: for instance, the first was called the 'Reich Party Congress of Victory', while with doubtless unintentional irony, the rally at which the Nuremberg Laws were enacted went by the name of the 'Reich Party Congress of Freedom'. The 1939 event, cancelled due to the outbreak of war, was to have been the 'Reich Party Congress of Peace'.

The International Military Tribunal was convened by the Allies in August 1945 in Nuremberg. Aside from its obvious symbolic value, the city was also chosen for the very practical reason that its large Palace of Justice complex, including an attached gaol, had largely survived extensive bombing.

Three Men and their Sheds

[British/Canadian: Anderson shelter/Morrison shelter/Nissen hut]

Fear of bombing was acute in the years leading up to the outbreak of war, although estimates of the deaths and casualties turned out to be wildly exaggerated. When the conflict seemed imminent, many moved from towns and cities to buy or rent in what the press advertisements called 'a safer zone' or 'a peaceful setting', euphemisms for places away from likely target areas. Those unable to move – the vast majority of the population – but who were able to afford £160 (more than £20,000 in today's money) might have had a private air raid shelter installed underground on their property. One builder in Watford offered a well-appointed shelter containing an 'emergency exit, air-conditioning plant and lavatory'. This was designed to hold up to seven people and the phrase 'proof against overcrowding' suggests that the owner would not be welcoming many of his neighbours.

The large-scale shelters, which have become familiar in the folk memory of World War Two, particularly those in the Underground stations, were not set up in the early stages of the conflict. The government was against them, partly on health and sanitary grounds, but mostly because it was believed that deep shelters would create a nation of defeatists and 'troglodytes'. Something had to be done, though, and the first response was the mass distribution of the Anderson shelter, named after John Anderson who was briefly Home Secretary (1939–40). The shelter, designed by William Paterson, a Scottish engineer, consisted of two curved walls of corrugated, galvanised steel which, together with end panels, was placed in a three-foot-deep pit in the garden, bolted together and then covered with earth. Because it was set into the the ground, cold, dampness and even flooding were inevitable problems. Yet, as the *New Statesman* reassuringly observed in the midsummer of 1939: 'Goats sheltered from high explosive in Anderson shelters were claimed to be quite unhurt.' If you didn't have a garden, then the suggestion was that you erect the Anderson in the kitchen. The shelters were distributed free to those on incomes of under £250 a year; otherwise you had to pay, albeit only a small fraction of what a privately built, air-conditioned set-up would have cost.

Even cheaper and simpler was the Morrison shelter, named after Herbert Morrison, the Home Secretary following John

Anderson. This protection against air raids was intended for indoor use and was, in effect, a glorified kitchen table. Topped with a steel plate and with wire mesh around the sides to guard against flying debris, the Morrison shelter also had springs in the base to support a mattress. Children often slept there as a matter of course, to be joined by parents in the event of a raid. It might have been a squeeze but it was dry, indoors and less uncomfortable than the Anderson, and had the advantage of being quicker to reach, something that was genuinely useful during the V-1 and V-2 campaigns of 1944/5 when the advance warning of any attack was much briefer. As with the Anderson shelter, the Morrison was provided free to those on low incomes; otherwise the cost was £7.

The cheapest and simplest option of all was to dig a shelter in the form of a trench or dugout in the back garden. Men who were veterans of World War One were familiar enough with what was required. And, if you had no garden or no war veteran to dig it, there was always the cupboard under the stairs. It was noticed that this refuge was sometimes the only place left intact in an otherwise pulverised suburban home.

The military equivalent of these quick-assembly structures was the Nissen hut, named after the Canadian mining engineer who invented it during World War One. The Nissen was made of curved sheets of corrugated iron bolted on a wooden frame and set on a concrete base. It was widely used for troop accommodation and storage, and not only during both world wars. Nissen huts are still a feature of the English landscape, converted to new uses, for example, on farmland. Crick and Watson's discovery of the double helix structure of DNA was made in old Nissen huts. The American equivalent of the Nissen was the Quonset hut, first made in 1941 and named after Quonset Point, a peninsula and one-time US Navy base in Rhode Island.

There is an obvious link between these relatively cheap, quick-to-build constructions and the boom in 'prefab' (prefabricated) housing, which occurred after the end of the war. In 1944, Winston Churchill announced plans to build half a million prefabs as part of the Temporary Housing Programme. About a third of that number was eventually constructed and quite a few of these 'detached bungalows' remain, especially around Bristol and in Newport, Wales, far exceeding the lifespan of a few years which was predicted for them.

A Defiant Detour

[German: *'Hauptstadt der Bewegung'* /
Drückebergergassl, the 'capital city of the
[National Socialist] movement',
i.e. Munich/Shirkers' Alley]

There is a short cobbled street in the centre of Munich called the Viscardigasse, which runs behind the Palais Preysing south of Odeonsplatz ('Odeon Square'). Backing onto the palace, and facing the square, is a 19th-century loggia known as the *Feldherrnhalle* ('Field Marshals' Hall'). It was outside this monumental building that Hitler's first attempt to seize power – the 'Beer Hall Putsch' – was brought to an abrupt and violent end on 9 November 1923. On their way to storm the Bavarian Defence Ministry, a group of 2,000 insurrectionists, led by Hitler, Goering and the World War One hero, Erich Ludendorff, came up against 100 armed police loyal to the Weimar Republic. The ensuing firefight left 16 Nazis and four policemen dead;* the would-be revolutionaries scattered.

When he became Chancellor a decade later, Hitler turned the *Feldherrnhalle* into a shrine for his fallen comrades, who became known in the hyperbolic parlance of Nazi propaganda as 'blood witnesses' (*Blutzeugen*). A plaque inscribed with their names and the legend *Und ihr habt doch gesiegt* ('You did triumph after all') was mounted on the eastern façade of the loggia, with an SS honour guard constantly in attendance. Anyone passing the site was required to give the straight-armed Nazi salute. To avoid paying homage, opponents of the regime simply took to walking behind the Palais Preysing and emerging onto Odeonsplatz on the west side of the *Feldherrnhalle* instead. This simple dodge earned the street its local nickname of 'Drückebergergassl' ('Shirkers' Alley'). In 1935, Hitler decreed that Munich should be given the honorary title of *Hauptstadt der Bewegung*, 'capital city of the movement'.

The plaque to the putschists was removed in 1945, and one commemorating the dead policemen was installed opposite the hall. In 'Shirkers' Alley' itself, the city authorities marked this small act of civil disobedience by setting a 30-metre S-shaped section of bronze cobblestones in the roadway in 1995.

*Hermann Goering was wounded in the leg, an injury that left him addicted to morphine for the rest of his life.

The Final Summit

[Russian: Yalta]

The summit conference in the Black Sea town of Yalta in February 1945 was the second and last time that the Big Three

– Roosevelt, Stalin and Churchill – met to fix the shape of the world before Germany's imminent defeat and the expected surrender of Japan. The remote Crimean venue, which had been badly damaged in the German retreat from the Ukraine, was Stalin's choice. Fearful of flying, he claimed that his earlier round trip from the Caspian city of Baku to Tehran for the summit conference of 1943 (the only occasion in his life when he flew) had caused him ear trouble. Eager to keep the Russian dictator onside, Churchill and Roosevelt agreed to travel to Yalta, a place which the British Prime Minister said might be survived with adequate supplies of whisky, which was 'good for typhus and deadly on lice which thrive in those parts'. The US went one step further by sending in a naval delousing team.

Whatever Stalin's neuroses, he was the least unfit of the three Allied leaders. Roosevelt was a mortally-ill man and died less than two months after the conclusion of the Yalta meeting. At 70, Churchill was the oldest of the three and had already caused anxiety to his family and entourage with various health problems including heart difficulties and bouts of pneumonia. More significant, though, was the marginalisation of the Prime Minister and the country he represented. Britain's finest hour and Churchill's too, when they stood alone against Nazi Germany, was by now several years in the past. The industrial might and global reach of the United States had turned that nation into the world's uncrowned superpower, while the Soviet Union – with its ruthless leadership, vast landmass and seemingly unlimited resources of men – was proving itself to be a force that must, in the end, grind through to victory. By contrast, Britain was an exhausted, overstretched and indebted island, a country whose influence consisted largely in its imperial legacy, the respect accorded to Churchill and admiration for the national defiance of 1939–41.

A total of 700 advisers, military and diplomatic, attended Yalta. Bedbugs abounded and bathroom conditions were primitive, but Russian hospitality was lavish. At one dinner, 45 toasts were drunk. When Roosevelt, greeting Stalin in the Tsarist palace which had been allotted to him, presented the dictator with a Martini – it was his habit to mix cocktails himself – he lamented the absence of lemon peel. The following morning there appeared outside a great tree with 200 lemons, flown in overnight from Georgia.

Perhaps the most telling feature of Yalta was the way in which the interests of lesser countries were ignored or, at best, lightly consulted while the US and the USSR planned the postwar dispensation. The biggest tussle was over the political make-up of the Polish government and the Polish frontiers, all dictated by non-Poles. The French weren't invited to Yalta even though they were to take control of one of the four zones in a defeated Germany. Churchill was kept in the dark about an exchange whereby, in return for Stalin's agreeing to enter the war against Japan, the Americans accepted the validity of some Russian territorial claims, particularly to the Kurile Islands (about which a dispute with Japan continues to this day), as well as other interests connected to China. Although Roosevelt had presciently seen China as one of the leaders of the postwar world – the 'Four Policemen' was his term – their leader, Chiang Kai-shek, was also kept ignorant of arrangements concerning his country. For their part the Americans settled some questions about the United Nations, to be inaugurated in San Francisco in April 1945, a project close to Roosevelt's heart.

Yalta has often been seen as a capitulation by the West to Stalin and as the almost shameful ushering-in of an era of Soviet dominance in Eastern Europe, a counterpart to the prewar Munich agreement with Hitler. As Jonathan Fenby says in his study of the wartime summits, *Alliance* (2006):

[Yalta] would be a key item on the McCarthyite charge sheet against Roosevelt, and lead to denunciations of secret betrayals by Republicans. Half a century later, George W. Bush declared in Warsaw: 'No more Munichs, no more Yaltas.'

Yet, as Fenby also points out, the shape of the post-1945 world could already be discerned before Yalta. Russia was the dominant force in Eastern Europe because the Red Army was there, 10-million strong, and Stalin had no intention of relinquishing control, whether it was attained by force or manipulation of the political process. People in the West were in no condition to contemplate another conflict with a fresh enemy; indeed, the Soviet Union was widely regarded as a heroic partner. Yalta was far from perfect but, as President Roosevelt said to a supporter. 'I didn't say the result was good. I said it was the best I could do.'

'Germany Calling'
[British: Lord Haw-Haw]

William Joyce (see also p. 144) made himself notorious through his voice, and it was his voice that in the end was to betray him. Born in 1906 in New York, of an Irish-American father and an English mother, Joyce returned with his family first to Ireland

and then to England. While at London University, Joyce joined the British Fascisti, formed in imitation of Mussolini's party. He transferred his allegiance to the Conservative Party before becoming Oswald Mosley's deputy in the British Union of Fascists. But Mosley wasn't anti-Semitic enough for Joyce and so he founded his own party, the National Socialist League (NSL), and advocated unity with Germany.

Shortly before the outbreak of war and knowing he would be interned, he travelled with his wife Margaret to Germany. Within a few days he was broadcasting on the *Reichsrundfunk*'s English-language service, airing propaganda designed to undermine the British war effort, cast slurs on Churchill, promote German moderation, and so on. The 'Lord Haw-Haw' nickname was originally applied in mockery by a *Daily Express* journalist to another plummy-voiced broadcaster from Germany but it soon stuck to William Joyce. In Berlin he became the leading voice of a mixed crew of English-speaking propagandists, including a Mrs Eckersley and her sixteen-year-old son Jimmy Clark as well as P.G. Wodehouse, the creator of Bertie Wooster and Jeeves. Listener research, commissioned by the BBC, found that Joyce's broadcasts were listened to more out of curiosity than defeatism. Margaret Joyce – inevitably, Lady Haw-Haw – had her own slot broadcasting weekly talks to British women. Joyce's style has been called both 'creepy' and 'jeering' and compared to that of a Hyde Park Corner ranter. Justifying his nickname, he had the educated, even affected tone of radio speakers familiar from the BBC of those days. (Snippets of his talks can be heard at the BBC Archives website.)

Some of the others faltered in their devotion to National Socialism but not Joyce, who continued to bang the drum of anti-Semitism, announcing his presence with the phrase 'Germany calling'. When staying in Berlin became impossible as the Allies advanced, transmissions came instead from Hamburg. From there, during a drunken ramble on 30 April 1945, Joyce's last words were 'Heil Hitler and farewell'. He and Margaret were discovered near the Danish border, where he was shot in the thigh and arrested after a British soldier recognised his voice. Although he had never held British nationality, Joyce was convicted of treason partly on the grounds that he owed allegiance to the Crown, having once possessed a British passport (fraudulently acquired by stating he was born in Ireland rather than the US). If justice was stretched to convict him, it was a measure of how despised he was. Lord Haw-Haw was hanged at Wormwood Scrubs on 3 January 1946.

Mrs Eckersley and Jimmy Clark were luckier: she was imprisoned for a year, while he was bound over to keep the peace for two years. Margaret Joyce was detained in military custody for some months but never charged. She died in Ireland in 1972.

Paean to a Pimp

[German: *Das Horst-Wessel-Lied;* the Horst Wessel Song]

The unofficial German national anthem during the Nazi period, and counterpart to Italian Fascism's *Giovinezza* (*see* Chapter 3: Lauding the *Duce*), was the *Horst-Wessel-Lied* ('Horst Wessel Song'). It was named after a Nazi storm trooper and early member of the party. Born the son of a Lutheran pastor in Berlin in 1907, Wessel became an activist for a monarchist political grouping at the age of 15, but soon gravitated even further to the right when he joined the nascent NSDAP in 1926. He was a shawm player and in 1929 wrote the words – though not the tune – for a new Nazi battle hymn, to be performed by the marching band of these raucous instruments that he had formed within the *Sturmabteilung* (SA) unit that he led. Originally entitled *Der unbekannte SA-Mann* ('The Unknown SA-Man'), this was the song that was later to immortalise his name. Its first verse ran:

Die Fahne hoch! die Reihen dicht geschlossen!
SA marschiert mit ruhig festem Schritt
Kam'raden, die Rotfront und Reaktion erschossen
Marschier'n im Geist in unsern Reihen mit.

['With flag held high and tightly closed ranks
The SA marches with a calm, determined step
Comrades whom the Red Front and reactionaries gunned
    down
March in spirit within our ranks.']

Later that same year, Wessel took up with a Berlin prosti-tute, Erna Jänicke; he moved into her flat and, having no other means of support, is thought to have lived off the immoral earnings he garnered as her procurer. Jänicke's landlady was a supporter of the Communist Party (KPD) and, when a dispute arose about unpaid rent, a local KPD enforcer called Albrecht Höhler came round to the apartment, got caught up in a violent argument with Wessel, and shot him in the face. The Nazi propaganda machine lost no time in proclaiming Wessel a *Blutzeuge* ('blood witness'), a martyr to the National Socialist cause. (Joseph Goebbels, in his role as *Gauleiter* of Berlin, had known the young man personally.) At Wessel's funeral, the Communists marked his passing by daubing the slogan *Dem Zuhälter Horst Wessel ein letztes Heil Hitler!* ('A final Heil Hitler to the pimp Horst Wessel!') on the cemetery wall.

Late in the war, as privations began to make ordinary Germans' lives a misery, the *vox pop* came up with a bitter spoof of the Horst-Wessel-Lied:

> *Die Preise hoch, die Läden fest geschlossen*
> *Die Not marschiert mit unentwegtem Schritt*
> *Und Adolf, Hermann, Joseph und Genossen*
> *Sie hungern – aber nur im Geiste mit!*

> ['With prices sky-high and all the shops closed
> Hardship marches steadily onward
> And Adolf, Hermann, Joseph and their comrades
> Are starving alongside us – but only in spirit!']

Living on in Infamy
[American: Pearl Harbor]

Tension between the United States and Japan was rising in 1941, with the Japanese determined on becoming the dominant power in East Asia and already engaged in war against China, a principal ally to the US under the nationalist leadership of Chiang Kai-shek. There were various motives behind the Pearl Harbor attack, which was, in effect, a declaration of war on America without any diplomatic ultimatum or warning. Denied oil imports from the US because of an embargo, Japanese military leaders knew that the fuel and other resources required to keep their forces supplied could be obtained from the Dutch East Indies. A southerly move to seize these assets would expose them to US naval and air power, something which could be forestalled by a surprise attack, preferably before America was able to complete a programme of reinforcement and airfield construction across the Pacific. In October 1941, the accession to power in Japan of General Tojo Hideki, who replaced a less militaristic Prime Minister, made war almost certain.

The attack on the US naval base on the Hawaiian island of Oahu occurred early on Sunday 7 December. Two waves of bombers and fighters killed over 3,500 servicemen and civilians, sunk six battleships and destroyed or damaged 12 other vessels and nearly 300 aircraft. Fearing a counter-attack, the Japanese commander did not order a third strike, which could – by destroying repair and refuelling facilities – have finished off Pearl Harbor as a base.

For President Roosevelt, the Sunday of Pearl Harbor was a 'date that will live in infamy'. On Monday 8 December, Congress approved the declaration of war on Japan with a single dissenting vote (from a Republican pacifist). Winston Churchill and Charles de Gaulle, leader of the Free French forces, saw the entry of the United States into the war as settling the outcome, whatever the battles and setbacks along the way. Hitler, too, welcomed Pearl Harbor. The daring quality of this attack appealed to him and, as *The Times* pointed out in an editorial, it was similar in its treachery and surprise to the assault on Russia begun in the summer of that year. The German dictator now had an ally on the other side of the world, and one who had not been defeated for thousands of years. On Friday 12 December, during a speech in Berlin, the dictator declared war on the US, claiming that he was pre-empting an attack which Roosevelt was planning on Germany and Italy.

'Pearl Harbor' rapidly entered the language not just in its own right but as a shorthand term for any overwhelming attack, combining surprise and deception; it is occasionally found in a rather cumbersome verb form ('to Pearl-Harbor'). The word and the still-fresh historical memory were immediately invoked following the Twin Towers attacks of 11 September 2001 in New York.

Tit for Tat

[German: *coventrieren;* 'to coventrate']

In the guise of the Francoist 'Condor Legion', the embryonic German Luftwaffe cut its teeth in the technique of carpet-bombing urban areas with its notorious raid on the undefended Basque town of Guernica in 1937, during the Spanish Civil War. The atrocity was immortalised in a huge painting by Pablo Picasso.

Three years later and Coventry, a major British manufacturing centre, was on the receiving end. Raids were conducted against the Midlands city from August 1940 onwards, the heaviest of which took place on the night of 14 November. Over 500 people were killed in this attack and the city was razed to the ground. So pleased were the Nazis with the results of 'Operation Moonlight Sonata' (so-called because a full 'bomber's moon' illuminated the target) that Joseph Goebbels immediately invented the verb *coventrieren*, 'to coventrate'; meaning to bomb intensively. Word soon reached Britain of this gloating coinage; on 21 December 1940, the *New Statesman* reported: 'The fact was that "coventrating" meant that the nerves and sinews and muscles of local government were wrenched and lacerated.'

The British were soon to repay the Germans in kind, with ever more massive night-time raids against major cities. The port of Hamburg was hit especially hard. After the devastating 'firestorm' attack on 27–28 July 1943 (*see* Chapter 9: A Terrible Prophecy), a new word duly entered the English language (*Brisbane Courier-Mail*, 21 September 1943): 'Hamburg, after the last four RAF night raids and American day raids, has nine square miles "Hamburgised".' Tit for tat, both militarily and linguistically.

After the war, Coventry twinned not with Hamburg but with the German city that came to epitomise the ultimate horror of area bombing: Dresden.

Perfidious Albion?
[French: Mers-el-Kébir]

Even today, the name of this naval base near the port city of Oran in Algeria can still touch a raw nerve in France, where it became a byword for the deadly treachery of its erstwhile ally and partner in the *Entente Cordiale*, Great Britain.

On 3 July 1940, barely a fortnight after France had sued for peace and concluded an armistice with Nazi Germany, a flotilla of Royal Navy vessels, including two battleships, a battlecruiser and an aircraft carrier, launched a devastating attack on the French fleet at anchor in the Algerian port. Continuing sporadically for five days, the bombardment ('Operation Catapult') resulted in the sinking of one French battleship, serious damage to five other capital ships, and the death of almost 1,300 French sailors. The British had feared

that their naval supremacy in the Mediterranean, safe-
guarding vital supply routes to Malta, Cyprus and Egypt and
already threatened by a powerful Italian fleet, would be
comprehensively lost if the assets of the French Navy should
fall into German hands. Although a clause in the armistice
signed by the Vichy government expressly forbade such an
act, Britain had little faith that this would be observed. British
commander, Vice-Admiral Sir James Somerville, presented
his French opposite number in Mers, Admiral Marcel
Gensoul, with three options: join forces and fight alongside
the British, surrender the fleet or sail to a French port in the
Caribbean, where the ships would be decommissioned. When
all options were rejected, on Churchill's direct instructions,
Somerville's task force opened fire.

The Mers-el-Kébir incident sharpened Anglophobe sentiment in France and handed the Axis a major propaganda coup.
The 19th-century spectre of *La perfide Albion* rose again;
posters went up showing a drowning French sailor above the
legend *N'oubliez pas Oran!* ('Remember Oran!') In a radio
broadcast from London on 8 July, Charles de Gaulle expressed
the anger and sorrow that he and his compatriots felt at *l'af-
freuse cannonade d'Oran* ('the dreadful bombardment at
Oran'), but stopped short of criticising his British hosts. Six
days later, addressing the House of Commons, Churchill spoke
of 'the sad duty of putting effectually out of action for the duration of the war the capital ships of the French Navy'.

The action remains highly contentious. While British historians tend to regard the attack as a necessary pre-emptive strike
by a beleaguered Britain *in extremis* after Dunkirk, the French
cite the scuttling of 77 naval vessels at Toulon in November 1942
to prevent their seizure by the Germans as evidence that they

would always have fulfilled their armistice duty not to let their fleet fall into the hands of any foreign nation.

The Swiss Fifth Column

[German: Wilhelm Gustloff]

While individual German spies were active in wartime Britain, fears of large-scale networks of Nazi sympathisers there proved groundless, especially after die-hard members of Oswald Mosley's British Union of Fascists were interned at the outbreak of hostilities. The situation was radically different, though, where a sizable German expatriate community could be tapped into. Hitler's fifth column was officially known as the NSDAP–AO: *Nazionalsozialistische Deutsche Arbeiterpartei– Auslandsorganisation*, or 'Overseas Organisation of the German National Socialist Workers' Party'. It was active in no fewer than 76 countries, and had the express aim of mobilising sympathisers among the five million or so Germans living abroad when the Nazis came to power; there was even a branch in the United States (*Gau Amerika*). But far and away its best-subscribed and most effective branch was in Switzerland, where the NSDAP began organising in the early 1930s. Quite apart from garnering support from Germanophone Swiss sympathisers of the fascist cause, the National Socialists had fertile soil in which to sow the seeds of internal unrest in the form of the largest colony of German expatriates in the whole of Europe (numbering around 100,000). Indeed, the Swiss branch of the party was founded in 1932 by Wilhelm Gustloff, a German national from the Baltic province of Mecklenburg who had come to Switzerland aged 22 in 1917 and settled in the ski resort of Davos, where he hoped the mountain air would

cure his chronic lung disease and laryngitis. Gustloff assidu-
ously built up a network of local party groups and youth
organisations in cities such as Zurich, Basle, and Lugano, and
by 1936 had an impressive roll-call of over 5,000 members. In
February of that year, however, his extended Alpine rest-cure
was drastically curtailed when he was shot four times in the
head by another expat, the Croatian medical student and
rabbi's son, David Frankfurter.*

Though the Nazi Party was outlawed in Switzerland in the
aftermath of Gustloff's assassination, covert organisation
continued under the cloak of legitimate diplomatic activity by
the German Consulate. As a none-too-subtle veiled threat,
when Germany mobilised for war, the 12,000–13,000 German
men of fighting age resident in Switzerland were not recalled to
the Fatherland to join the colours, but were left in situ. In May
1940, Hitler specifically instructed his Propaganda Minister,
Joseph Goebbels, to let the German press use the term 'Fifth
Column' (*Fünfte Kolonne*) in order to foment unease and
mistrust in the 'enemy nations'. It is a moot point whether the
Führer viewed Switzerland in such a light. In the event, surveillance of potential insurrectionists both by Swiss government
agencies and secretly-organised civilian self-defence commit-
tees helped neutralise any threat. Cynics might also contend
that Hitler and his confederates were well aware that the
'Gnomes of Zurich' – as investors in German industry and
discreet offshore bankers of looted Jewish treasure – were far
better left alone to get on with their nefarious business than
invaded.

*Two years later, when another young Jewish man dared to assassi-
nate a Nazi functionary on foreign soil (Herschel Grynszpan's
shooting of diplomat Ernst von Rath in Paris), the incident was used in

Germany as a pretext for the murderous mass assault on synagogues and Jewish homes and business that came to be known as *Kristallnacht* ('crystal' was an allusion to the resulting mountains of broken glass). On the occasion of Gustloff's killing, however, the Nazis largely confined themselves to ostentatious displays of grief. A lavish state funeral was laid on in his hometown of Schwerin (the train carrying the body from Davos made several stops at German cities en route for devotees to pay their respects), and Gustloff was declared a *Blutzeuge* of the movement. Most notably, a brand-new cruise ship of the Nazi 'Strength Through Joy' workers' recreational organisation (*see* Chapter 3: Workers' Playtime – German Style), which was due to be named *Adolf Hitler*, was rechristened the *Wilhelm Gustloff* when it was launched in May 1937. The vessel proved as ill-fated as its human namesake, being torpedoed with massive loss of life in early 1945. Interested readers are referred to Günter Grass's gripping account of the tragedy in his 2002 novella *Im Krebsgang* ('Crabwalk').

Chapter 14

Racial Policy and Genocide

In 2001, in an attempt to emulate the recent runaway success of British inventor James Dyson's 'Dual Cyclone' vacuum cleaner, the Bosch Siemens company approached the US Patent & Trademark Office to register the German equivalent – *Zyklon* – for a range of its home appliances. A storm of protest erupted, and the firm was forced to withdraw its application. The offending word, which recalled the insecticide used in the gas chambers of Auschwitz and other death camps – *Zyklon B* – is one of several terms so tainted by associations with the Third Reich that they are shunned in modern German discourse. They almost all relate to Nazi racial theory and the ensuing Holocaust. Other notorious examples are *Endlösung* (the 'final solution' of the 'Jewish problem', i.e. their extermination) and *entartet* ('degenerate', a word borrowed from the pseudoscience of eugenics).

The language of racial hatred underwent a shift during the twelve years of Nazi rule, moving from vituperative metaphors likening the Jews to vermin, parasites and diseases to chilling bureaucratic euphemisms, which couched different aspects of the business of mass murder in terms of 'resettlement', 'selection' and 'special treatment'.

Marked out for Murder

[**German:** *der gelbe Fleck,* 'the Yellow Patch'
(i.e. Jewish Star)]

In 1936, a collection of reports by journalists exposing the campaign of violence directed at Germany's Jews since Hitler's accession to power was published in Paris, with a foreword by the renowned German-Jewish writer, Lion Feuchtwanger (author of the highly successful historical novel *Jew Süss*), who by then was living in exile in the south of France. Its title and subtitle were *Der gelbe Fleck: Die Ausrottung von 500.000 deutschen Juden* ('The Yellow Patch: The extermination of 500,000 German Jews'). The book's authors painted a compelling picture of officially orchestrated discrimination and murder. Despite this, that renowned paragon of moral probity, the IOC, failed to rescind its decision to hold the Summer Olympic Games in Berlin later that year.

The cover of the book depicted a plain yellow circle, an allusion to the 'rotella' that was extensively used during the Middle Ages to mark out Jews from their compatriots in many European realms.* The prime mover in this act of segregation was the Catholic Church; Canon 68 of the Fourth Lateran Council of 1215 explicitly called for distinguishing dress so as to divest practitioners of 'prohibited intercourse' between Jews and Gentiles of any excuse that they were unaware of the racial background of their partner. In the Third Reich, although such a measure was first mooted in 1938, it was 1941 before the Yellow Patch was introduced throughout Nazi Europe. It took the form of a Star of David with the word 'Jew' displayed prominently in the centre, in faux-Hebrew lettering, in either German or the language of the occupied territory concerned

185

(thus, *Juif* in France, *Jood* in the Netherlands, and so on).**
The Nazis' intentions went far beyond the prevention of inter-
racial sexual congress; that had already been proscribed by one
of the Nuremberg Laws of 1935, the *Gesetz zum Schutz des
deutschen Blutes und der deutschen Ehre* ('Law for the
Protection of German Blood and German Honour'). Joseph
Goebbels made the regime's sinister intentions plain in an
editorial in the weekly newspaper *Das Reich* on November 16,
1941:

> *Anyone wearing the Jewish Star is thereby clearly identi-
> fied as an enemy of the people.*

In a fascinating prefiguring of the African-American community's re-appropriation of the 'N-word', wresting it away from its
use as a racial slur by white supremacists, a journalist named
Robert Weltsch wrote a leader in 1933 exhorting his fellow
Jews to treat the very symbol used to discriminate against
them as a point of pride. In the article, entitled *Tragt ihn mit
Stolz, den gelben Fleck!* ('Wear the Yellow Patch with Pride!'),
Weltsch cited the daubing by storm troopers of Stars of David
on Jewish businesses to be boycotted, and concluded:

> *The Jews, under attack, must learn to acknowledge them-
> selves . . . one often saw windows bearing a large Magen
> David, the Shield of David the King. It was intended as
> dishonour. Jews, take it up, the Shield of David, and wear
> it with pride!*

Tragically, no amount of defiant cultural self-affirmation could
save the Jews of occupied Europe from the Hitler regime's

programme of genocide. Some six million were to perish before the war's end.

*The origin of the colour yellow for these 'marks of shame' is uncertain. Some claim that, in medieval colour symbolism, yellow had distinctly negative connotations, being associated with greed and envy, as well as poison or pestilence. Alternatively, it may simply have been used because it was highly visible.

**Some German-Jewish wearers of the yellow star indulged in gallows humour, claiming that they had been awarded the *Pour le Sémite* (a pun on the Kingdom of Prussia's highest award, the *Pour le Mérite*).

France's Shame

[French: *la rafle,* round-up/police swoop]

Films ranging from Marcel Ophuls's masterly documentary *Le Chagrin et la Pitié* ('The Sorrow and the Pity; 1971) to Jacques Audiard's contentious drama *Un héros très discret* ('A Self-Made Hero'; 1996) reflect the deep rifts that ran through French society in the Vichy period and the postwar Fourth Republic. On the credit side of France's war ledger was the astonishing courage shown by the men and woman of the Resistance in their guerrilla campaign against both the Germans and the hated Vichy *Milice*; on the debit side was the shocking speed with which the country's armed forces had collapsed during the invasion, capitulating after barely six weeks of fighting in May–June 1940.

Yet, undoubtedly, the most shameful and tragic episode in the history of occupied France took place on 16–17 July 1942. From four o'clock on the morning of the first day, police units began to round up the entire Jewish population of the Greater Paris area, estimated at 22,000 people. Many of them had fled from Eastern Europe and taken refuge in France. By the end of the operation, over 13,000 men, women and children had been arrested; most were taken in buses to a makeshift holding camp in a covered cycle racetrack in the 15th *arrondissement* near the Eiffel Tower. This notorious incident takes its name from that arena, the *Rafle du Vélodrome d'Hiver* (usually abbreviated to *Rafle du Vel d'Hiv*; 'The Winter Velodrome Round-up'). For five to seven days, the detainees were kept there in cramped and insanitary conditions; all the toilets had been boarded up, as their windows offered a potential means of escape. Subsequently, the Jews were transferred to the main internment facility at Drancy north of Paris and thence to Auschwitz. The numbers seized in the *Rafle* accounted for more than a sixth of all the Jews deported from France to Germany for extermination in the war. Only 50 of the original 13,152 are believed to have survived.

Although the swoop (code-named *Opération Vent printanier*, 'Operation Spring Breeze') was planned in conjunction with the SS, its chief architects were the Vichy French officials René Bousquet and Louis Darquier de Pellepoix. The former received a trifling sentence at the end of the war for collaboration while the latter evaded justice by fleeing to Franco's Spain. Furthermore, the operation was executed solely by a force of 9,000 French police supplemented by youth members of the fascist *Parti Populaire Français* (PPF). In other words, the *Rafle* was an almost entirely homegrown hate crime. A monument was erected in 1994 near the site of the velodrome (which burned down in 1959), and a year later President Jacques Chirac finally acknowledged the complicity of organs of the French state in this monstrous act of genocide.

Glossing over Genocide

[**German:** *Sprachregelung/Umsiedlung/*
Evakuierung, **'Prescribed terminology'/**
'Relocation'/'Evacuation':
euphemisms for mass murder]

These days, we are wise to mealy-mouthed euphemisms. The newspeak of current business terminology abounds in them. Take 'rationalisation', 'downsizing' and 'restructuring'. All these circumlocutions boil down to a single unpalatable truth: droves of expendable minions have been earmarked for redundancy while senior management will, as always, remains unscathed and overpaid.

But all that pales into insignificance beside history's most obscene charade of official mendacity: Nazi Germany's attempts to dress up the transportation of Europe's Jews to the death camps as something other than mass murder on an industrial scale. There was even a word for it: *Sprachregelung* – literally 'language regulation', i.e. prescribed terminology.*

On 19 July, 1942 the head of the SS Heinrich Himmler ordered the 'relocation' (*Umsiedlung*) of all Jews resident in the Polish General Government (a large area of central and southern Poland, including the cities of Warsaw and Krakow, that had not become part of 'Greater Germany' but was under Nazi occupation) to concentration camps established in the east of Poland. The first three of these were Belzec, Sobibor and Treblinka. The action was known as 'Operation Reinhard' or 'Operation Reinhardt', with the varying spelling giving rise to disagreement among historians as to whether the code word was named after Himmler's deputy, Reinhard Heydrich, or German Secretary of State for Finance, Fritz Reinhardt.

Whatever the niceties of its name, between its inception and October 1943, this single programme resulted in the forced transportation and deaths of over two million Polish Jews and an estimated 50,000 Roma people.

Another seemingly innocuous term that was common currency in Nazi Germany for the central policy of genocide was *Evakuierung* ('evacuation'). The monthly report for May 1942 by the district president of Upper and Central Franconia (Bavaria) includes the chillingly matter-of-fact sentence:

> *On 24 March 781, and on 25 April 105 Jews were evacuated to the East. Aside from a few suicides and attempted suicides, the whole operation ran smoothly.*

As a way of quelling potential unrest, collaborationist governments adopted the same approach. The Vichy régime in France, for example, regularly referred to '*réinstallation* (or *transportation*) *à l'Est*'.

Lest we imagine that such doublespeak is the preserve of totalitarian regimes, it is worth recalling that after Pearl Harbor the US administration interned around 110,000 people of Japanese heritage who lived along the Pacific Coast in 'War Relocation Camps'. Yellow notices pinned to telephone poles announced implementation of the forced removal in the universal and timeless argot of uncaring bureaucracy:

> *Pursuant to the provision of Civilian Exclusion Order No. 92, this Headquarters, dated May 23, 1942, all persons of Japanese ancestry, both aliens and non-aliens [i.e. naturalized Japanese-Americans] will be evacuated from the*

above area by 12 o'clock noon, P.W.T., Saturday, May 30, 1942.

RJF RIP: Laying the Soap Myth to Rest

[**German:** *Reichsstelle für industrielle Fettversorgung (RIF),*
'State Agency for Industrial Fat Supply']

In *The Black Book of Russian Jewry*, one of the earliest compilations of survivor accounts of the Holocaust, which was assembled by the writers Ilya Ehrenburg and Vasily Grossman in 1944–5, a chilling atrocity is recorded:

In another section of the Belzec camp was an enormous soap factory. The Germans picked out the fattest people, murdered them, and boiled them down for soap.

Though presented as documentary fact, this notorious practice was actually an urban myth, deriving from a piece of black propaganda originally put about by the British in the Great War, and spread by the Germans themselves in World War Two to terrify camp inmates and keep them compliant.

In April 1917, British newspapers carried lurid stories of factories in Germany – whose economy was indeed by then in a desperate state – rendering human battlefield corpses, chiefly their own fallen soldiers, into fat to be used in the manufacture of soap. These *Kadaververwertungsanstalten* ('corpse reclamation facilities') certainly existed, but only ever processed animal carcasses. Foreign Secretary Austen Chamberlain finally acknowledged the falsehood of the rumour in 1925.

191

A seemingly strong piece of evidence corroborating the fear that the Nazis really were visiting this ghastly fate upon the victims of the 'Final Solution' was the set of initials stamped on bars of soap during the war. They were thought to read 'RJF', which popular wisdom maintained was short for *Rein Jüdisches Fett* ('Pure Jewish Fat'). But in old German *Fraktur* ('blackletter') script, the capitals 'J' and 'I' are almost indistinguishable; in fact, the abbreviation was 'RIF', which stood for *Reichsstelle für industrielle Fettversorgung* ('State Agency for Industrial Fat Supply'). The rumour had considerable mileage, though; the Yad Vashem Holocaust Memorial Centre in Jerusalem, which follows mainstream scholars in believing the story to be a fabrication, holds images of solemn postwar 'burials' of cakes of soap by the Romanian Jewish community and others.

While the soap-from-body-parts industry never existed, another one – the crafting and dissemination of conspiracy theories on the Internet – is booming. The real damage wrought by the soap myth has been to supply grist to the Holocaust deniers' mill of perceived injustices. This and another infamous, yet equally spurious, horror story of Nazi atrocity* have become totemic for the Far Right, which brandishes them as glaring examples of what it claims is a sustained campaign of vilification of the Third Reich.

*The rumour that patches of tattooed skin were cut from the bodies of inmates at the Buchenwald extermination camp and made into lampshades by Ilse Koch, the wife of the commandant. A fascinating exploration of this urban myth is given in a 2010 book by US author Mark Jacobson, *The Lampshade: A Holocaust Detective Story from Buchenwald to New Orleans.*

Spirited Away

[German: *Nacht-und-Nebel Erlaß*,
'Night and Fog Decree']

Sunday 7 December 1941 will always be remembered, first and foremost, for Japan's surprise attack on Pearl Harbor. But on that same date, Japan's wartime ally Nazi Germany committed arguably as momentous an act of war, in the passing of the *Nacht-und-Nebel-Erlaß* ('Night and Fog Decree'). This was the code name given to a directive issued by Hitler and signed by the Supreme Commander of the Armed Forces, Field Marshal Wilhelm Keitel, which instructed Germany's security services – the Gestapo and the *Sicherheitsdienst* (SD) – to seize anyone suspected of subversive activities throughout the occupied territories and deport them to the Fatherland for trial by special military courts. Like the notorious practice in our time of 'special rendition' in George W. Bush's 'War on Terror', this decree circumvented not only standard military procedure, but also the provisions of international law and various conventions governing the treatment of prisoners of war. In most cases, relatives of the 'disappeared' never found out what became of them.

In German, the common alliterative phrase '*bei Nacht und Nebel*' (literally 'by night and fog') denotes something done especially clandestinely, under cover not just of darkness but of a pea-souper too. What better way of conveying the sinister idea of spiriting a person away without anyone's knowledge?

The idiom's origins are, to risk a pun, lost in the mists of time. But undoubtedly its most (in)famous usage is in the libretto of Richard Wagner's opera *Das Rheingold*, the first of the four works that make up the Ring Cycle. In scene three, the dwarf

Alberich, guardian of the treasure of the Nibelungs, concealed under a 'magic helmet' (*Tarnhelm*) that acts like a cloak of invisibility, softly utters the words '*Nacht und Nebel. Niemand gleich*' – usually translated loosely as 'Night and darkness. Nowhere seen!' – to describe his position. Heated debate still rages around the question of Wagner and the Nazis, and here is not the place to revive it. Suffice it to say that Hitler was probably thinking of the opera when he coined the code name: the combination of the *völkisch* Germanic mysticism of the story and Wagner's bombastic realisation of the *Gesamtkunstwerk* ('total work of art') was tailor-made to chime in with Nazism's world view.

Secrecy continued to surround the fate of prisoners taken in the raids that followed the decree. Dispatched to concentration camps after trial, they wore jackets bearing the initials 'NN' and were singled out for particularly harsh treatment. The death rate among these inmates was very high. When SD records were examined after the war, the acronym 'NN' was likewise all that was noted next to certain names. In 1955, French director Alain Resnais made a renowned documentary film about the Nazi death camps, to which he gave the title *Nuit et brouillard*, in direct allusion to the directive. To emphasise the point, one of its most powerful sequences shows trains of deportees arriving through the gateway of Auschwitz-Birkenau in precisely those atmospheric conditions.

Homilies of Hatred

[German: *Jedem das Seine/Arbeit Macht Frei,*
'To Each His Own'/'Work Sets You Free']

The most appropriate motto for the National Socialists to have placed at the gates of their concentration camps would surely have been the famous line from Dante's *Inferno*: 'Abandon all hope, ye who enter here.' Yet, in a gesture emblematic of this monstrously inhumane regime, they chose instead two moralising sentiments whose sadistic mockery still has the power to elicit a *frisson* of disbelieving horror: *Jedem das Seine* and *Arbeit macht frei*.

As with the goose-step (*see* Chapter 6: 'A Horrible Sight'), it comes as a real surprise to learn that neither of these slogans originated with the Nazis. *Jedem das Seine* began life as the Latin dictum *suum cuique* ('To Each his Own'); in 19th-century Prussia, it appeared on the state's highest order of chivalry, the 'Order of the Black Eagle'. In that context, the motto could be read as the apotheosis of the Protestant work ethic. To paraphrase: merit comes to those who have earned it. But when incorporated into the wrought-iron gate of the concentration camp at Buchenwald, one of the earliest such facilities, which opened in 1937, it took on the quite different sense of 'Everyone will get his (or her) just deserts'. In other words, serves you right for being a Jew, a Slav, a Roma, a socialist or a homosexual.*

The second slogan was still more sinister. Above the gates to several of the murder-mills, including Sachsenhausen, Dachau, Flossenbürg, Theresienstadt and Auschwitz I, stood the legend *Arbeit Macht Frei* ('Work Sets you Free'). Though reminiscent of the Latin *Labor omnia vincit* ('Work overcomes everything', from Virgil's *Georgics*), the German phrase is in fact of more recent provenance: a 1998 study by the academic Wolfgang Brückner traced its first use back to the title of an 1872 novel by a German philologist, Lorenz Diefenbach, which tells of the redemption of miscreants through honest labour. Thereafter, the Weimar government adopted it as a motto for their public-works initiatives to alleviate mass unemployment (a counterpart to Roosevelt's 'New Deal'). Once again, its use by the Nazis can only be ascribed to a base desire to mock and humiliate their victims; far from ever attaining their freedom, countless thousands of prisoners were literally worked to death.** There remains the possibility – at least according to the German historian Martin Broszat and the German-American journalist Otto Friedrich – that the infamous camp commandant Rudolf Höss, the man responsible for installing the sign at Auschwitz, may have entertained a naïve notion that a regime of hard labour was spiritually liberating. In the end, of course, it would have been a matter of complete indifference to the inmates in Höss's charge whether their tormentor was a pious fantasist or just a cruel psychopath.

*With unconscious irony, the notion of 'To Each his Own' resurfaced in the euphemism used by Nazism's ideological heir, the white supremacist regime in South Africa (1948–94), to describe its central policy of *apartheid*: 'separate development of the races.' **The only explicit mention in official Nazi documents of the programme of systematic annihilation of prisoners came in a report of 18 September 1942 by Reich Justice Minister Otto Thierack summarising a conversation with Himmler, in which the two men had agreed on a policy of *Vernichtung durch Arbeit* ('extermination through work').

Chapter 15

Aftermath

World War Two shaped the path of the decades that followed 1945 and continues, though more distantly, to do so to this day. Linguistically, expressions out of that period survive and even thrive, from the most casual pieces of slang to the darkest of genocidal terms. On the political level, the changed world order which was already emerging in the closing stages of the war – a ravaged Europe and a supremely confident America facing down a would-be Soviet superpower – generated fresh words and phrases.

Twelve Guilty Men

[American/British: Nuremberg Trials/genocide]

The concept of war crimes was given impetus and a much wider definition by the trials in Nuremberg, a city chosen as the symbolic locale where key Nazi leaders would be held to account (*see* Chapter 13: Rallying Point). The scale of wartime atrocities reached the point where a completely new word would be required. Not recorded as occurring in English before 1944, 'genocide' was defined by the *Sunday Times* at the beginning of the Nuremberg process:

> *The United Nations' indictment of the 24 Nazi leaders has brought a new word into the language – genocide. It*

occurs in Count 3, where it is stated that all the defendants
'conducted deliberate and systematic genocide – namely,
the extermination of racial and national groups . . .'.

The decision to prosecute (Nazi) war crimes had been taken by the British, American and Russian leaders as early as 1943 but the form of the special tribunal to oversee the trials was not established until the end of the war. Older types of war crime such as the mistreatment of prisoners-of-war had long been defined in the Geneva and Hague Conventions, but the added categories were crimes against humanity and crimes against international peace. It was this first new category, including the mass murder of civilians, racial persecution and policies of extermination, which provided the rationale for the twelve death sentences passed at Nuremberg. Of these, eleven were carried out, since Hermann Goering escaped the hangman by swallowing cyanide only hours before his execution; nevertheless, his corpse joined the others laid out in a gymnasium for photographic record before being transported to an unknown location for cremation.

The Nuremberg Trials, which began on October 1945 and lasted for a year, were vulnerable to accusations of 'victor's justice'. Some of the charges, such as 'wanton destruction of cities', were soft-pedalled because the Allies had produced at least equivalent results with carpet-bombing. The elephant in the room was actually the Soviet bear, with prosecutors from one totalitarian regime pressing charges on the leaders of another. Nevertheless, Nuremberg became synonymous with an honourable, if flawed, attempt to hold individuals to account and to establish new laws relating to wars of aggression and genocide. War crimes trials covering the conflict in the Pacific were also held in Tokyo, although this process did not start until May 1948.

Swords into Ploughshares?
[American/German: The Morgenthau Plan/
der Nero-Befehl, 'the Nero Order']

In 1965, General Curtis LeMay, former commander of the US Strategic Air Command (SAC), retired from 35 years of eventful service and, as high-ranking military men often do, immediately published his autobiography. In a passage on the Vietnam War, which by then was sucking in ever larger numbers of American personnel, LeMay proposed a characteristically hawkish solution: '. . . they've [i.e. the North Vietnamese] got to draw in their horns and stop their aggression, or we're going to bomb them back into the Stone Age.' LeMay was no stranger to controversy: his bellicose opposition to Kennedy's sensitive handling of the Cuban Missile Crisis had earned him screen immortality when director Stanley Kubrick took him as the real-life model for Colonel Jack D. Ripper, the insane SAC base commander whose itchy trigger finger precipitates a thermonuclear war with Russia in *Dr Strangelove* (1964). But the 'Stone Age' remark took its place in a litany of hyperbole that henceforth became the US military and State Department's stock-in-trade. In 2006, Pakistani president Pervez Musharraf claimed that Deputy Secretary of State Richard Armitage had revived LeMay's notorious phrase to threaten his country if it failed to sever links with the Taliban; 10 years earlier, policymakers at the National Defense University formulated the grandiose doctrine of 'Shock and Awe', enacted in 2003 in the invasion of Iraq.

It's a seductive thought, bombing your adversary's infra-structure back into a prehistoric state. And yet, for all the heavy damage inflicted upon Nazi Germany's cities and populace by the RAF and the US Eighth Air Force, prior to the A-bomb air power lacked the means of delivering the *coup de grâce* to a nation's military-industrial complex. Conventional weapons yields were too small and targeting too inaccurate to achieve this, despite the claim made by the manufacturer of the USAAF's Norden bombsight that it could 'put a bomb in a pickle barrel from 20,000 feet' (more American hyperbole).

If you want to wreak real havoc, best leave it to a civil servant. In 1944, when discussing Germany's postwar 'industrial disar-mament', the Allies adopted a plan drawn up by US Treasury Secretary Henry Morgenthau, Jr. which envisaged the parti-tioning of the country and the wholesale destruction of its industrial base. In effect, Germany was to be reduced to an economy 'primarily agricultural and pastoral in its capacity'. Not prehistory, but definitely tantamount to a forced reversion to the Middle Ages. Understandably perhaps, after German militarism had caused two global conflicts within a quarter of a century, the rationale behind this thinking was to divest the country of its ability ever to wage war again. The Morgenthau Plan thus explicitly referred to the Ruhr region, then as now the heartland of German heavy industry, as a 'cauldron of wars'.

In the event, common sense prevailed and, not wishing to repeat the mistakes of 1919 and give a new generation of Germans a *casus belli* for renewed hostility in past grievances (*see* Chapter 1: Hitler's Whopper), the Allies opted for their former enemy to receive Marshall Aid and rebuild its industrial capacity. The result is the stable, democratic and economically robust Germany we see today. But in a bizarre postscript, it is worth noting that, had Morgenthau's plan ever been implemented, much of the groundwork for the destruction of Germany's modern infrastructure would have been laid by Adolf Hitler himself. On 19 March 1945, the Führer issued what was termed the 'Decree Relating to Demolition Measures on Reich Territory' (*Befehl betreffend Zerstörungsmaßnahmen im Reichsgebiet*). On one level, this was a 'scorched earth' policy aimed at depriving the advancing Allies of any succour. But on another, it confirmed that Hitler had, by then, consigned his own people to oblivion for being too 'weak' to realise his epochal master plan. Some factories were dynamited, and several kilometres of railway track torn up, but the decree was never fully enacted because Albert Speer, Minister of Armaments and War Production, was appalled at his leader's megalomania and deliberately dragged his feet. Two months later, Hitler was dead, Germany had surrendered, and the long task of rebuilding could begin. Significantly, Hitler's destructive decree is not remembered by its cumbersome official title; instead, recalling an earlier madman hell-bent on bringing the whole house down around his ears, it is simply known as the 'Nero Order'.

A Whiter Wash

[German: *ein Persilschein, 'a Persil certificate'*]

To the Allied occupying powers postwar fell the tricky task of de-Nazifying German society. Those Nazi big fish who had been netted when the Third Reich collapsed were swiftly brought to book at the Nuremberg trials (*see* Chapter 13: Rallying Point), but arguably a more difficult proposition was deciding which of the smaller fry who had joined the NSDAP were culpable enough to warrant further attention. The extent to which the German populace as a whole was complicit in the regime's crimes is still the subject of fierce debate; for example, Daniel Goldhagen's 1996 book *Hitler's Willing Executioners: Ordinary Germans and the Holocaust* argues that anti-Semitism ran far deeper than the upper echelons of the Nazi state.

The process began with all Germans being required to fill out a questionnaire of 10 sections, covering such matters as membership of official organisations and any speeches given or publications produced during the Nazi period. The collection and evaluation of these forms soon overwhelmed Allied bureaucracy, even the Americans with their state-of the-art Hollerith-IBM data machine, a precursor of the computer which used punched-card technology.

Presently, responsibility was devolved to the embryonic West German state, with the passing of the 'Law No. 104 for Liberation from National Socialism and Militarism' on 5 March 1946. Citizens applying for any form of public office were vetted. To speed up this laborious task, tribunals accepted character references from third parties exonerating suspected individuals; those written by former prisoners or political opponents carried more weight. Even so, the popular perception was that several functionaries who knew which strings to pull had been effectively 'whitewashed' by these affidavits, earning them the name of *Persilscheine*, 'Persil certificates', a reference to the detergent manufactured by the Henkel company of Düsseldorf since the early 1900s.

Summary Justice

In a sequence from director Marcel Ophuls's gripping documentary on French collaboration and resistance *Le Chagrin et la Pitié* ('The Sorrow and the Pity'; 1971), Mme. Solange, a hairdresser from Clermont-Ferrand, describes the rough justice that was meted out to her at the Liberation. Solange, a woman of Pétainist sympathies, was accused of having denounced a Resistance fighter; the interview is preceded by footage of women having their heads shaved in the street for so-called '*collaboration horizontale*' (i.e., consorting with German soldiers), a common punishment in France in 1944–5.*

These acts were part of the *épuration sauvage*, the spasm of retribution that overtook France as the German occupation came to an end and the Vichy government collapsed. The public humiliation of women suspected of having been 'Boche mattresses' (often unfairly; many prostitutes who had served both German and French clients were also assaulted) was just one aspect of a widespread vigilantism. Lynchings took place throughout the country; it is estimated that some 7,300 people were summarily executed by their compatriots. De Gaulle took urgent steps to bring this painful bloodletting to a close, instituting the *épuration legale* – due judicial process against collaborationists – in early 1945.

Motives for exacting revenge on fellow Frenchmen and Frenchwomen were many and varied, ranging from righteous anger at the death of a relative during the occupation to perverse attempts to expiate or conceal personal complicity. It could even boil down to petty jealousy. British journalist Alistair Horne, then serving with the Coldstream Guards, noted on the arrest of the French film star and singer Arletty, who had taken the Luftwaffe officer Hans-Jürgen Soehring as her lover '... what was held against her was not so much that she had slept with a German senior officer as that she had dined with him at the Ritz when other Parisians went hungry.' Arletty herself took a relaxed view of her actions: 'My heart is French,' she later coolly announced, 'but my ass is international.'

*The corresponding insult directed at women on the German-occupied Channel Islands who had slept with the enemy was 'Jerrybag'.

Voice of the People
[British: Mass Observation]

The idea behind reality TV and fly-on-the-wall documentaries is not new. In January 1937 a letter to the left-leaning magazine *New Statesman and Nation* announced the setting up of 'Mass Observation' and appealed for volunteers to report on everyday life, sometimes in its most minute or curious aspects. Among the subjects which might be addressed were: the behaviour of people at war memorials; the shouts and gestures of motorists; beards, armpits, eyebrows; anti-Semitism; and funerals and undertakers. The trio behind Mass Observation weren't sociologists but something odder and more bohemian. Charles Madge was a poet and communist, Humphrey Jennings a surrealist painter who later became a distinguished documentary film-maker, while Tom Harrisson was an anthropologist who, in 1945, parachuted into Borneo to lead headhunting tribes into guerrilla action against the Japanese.

The purpose of Mass Observation, the results of which were obtained through one-day diaries, questionnaires and direct reporting, was to chart the 'weather-maps of public feeling'. It was observation of the mass but also *by* the mass; the original ambition was for 5,000 observers. One of the events which prompted its creation was the 1936 Abdication Crisis when Edward VIII gave up the throne because he wanted to marry his twice-divorced American lover, Wallis Simpson. The public had been kept ignorant of what was going on until the last moment and there was a gap between popular feeling, which was pro-Edward, and the official establishment view. A 'Mass Observation' on 12 May 1937 – the day on which Edward's brother, the Duke of York, was crowned as George VI – provided a snapshot of 'real' opinions and behaviour, right down to subversive details like the Westminster Abbey usher who sneaked a cigarette in the King's state coach during the coronation service.

During the war the government hired Mass Observation to ascertain the views of the man (and woman) in the street and to check on morale. It was discovered that before the Blitz began, the blackout was unpopular because people thought it was pointless and, in addition, feared that their pets might be stolen. A propaganda poster with only a crown for illustration and proclaiming that victory would be achieved through '*Your* Courage, *Your* Cheerfulness, *Your* Resolution' went down very badly (*see* Chapter 10: The Popular Poster That Never Was). *Our* Courage, etc. would have been more appropriate. The Mass Observation findings were a vital complement to the research and polling carried out by the branch of the Ministry of Information known as Home Intelligence. Although the three men who founded Mass Observation fell out with each other, their brainchild was one of the precursors of contemporary polling and market research.*

The need to find out what ordinary people were thinking, what they felt and wanted, especially among the working class, was one of the key features of the 1930s and 1940s. This was not just middle-class discomfort over the effects of the economic slump that began with the Wall Street Crash of 1929, but a reflection of what was happening internationally. Soviet Russian was, in theory, a workers' state while the national socialism and fascism of Germany and Italy were nothing if not mass movements. So finding out about the 'masses' was vital to the work of government as well as being a project of intrinsic interest. Works of reportage from the working-class such as George Orwell's *Down and Out in Paris and London* (1933) and *The Road to Wigan Pier* (1937) had shown the way. Mass Observation followed, but it was essentially a snapshot rather than a representative and systematic survey. It was the US statistician George Gallup (1901–84) who pioneered the scientific method in the 1930s, and his surname soon became synonymous with opinion polls and electoral predictions. As early as 1940, the *Illustrated London News* was citing a Gallup poll by which 'President Roosevelt is assured of a total of 410 electoral votes.' Even before the election took place, the people had spoken.

*The Mass Observation records (from 1937 to the early 1950s) are curated by Sussex University. The 'citizen journalists' scheme was restarted in 1981.

State of Stasis

[American/British: Cold War]

The overriding need to fight against a common enemy meant that strains and disagreements among the Allies – principally, between Soviet Russia and the Western Allies – were glossed over until Germany and Japan were securely defeated. The Russian contribution to the war effort, and Stalin's leadership of it, were simply too vital to be undermined. Historians have placed the beginnings of the Cold War as far back as the formation of the Grand Alliance in 1941, even though the term did not gain general currency until the 1950s.

It was George Orwell who first used the expression 'cold war' to describe a state of hostility between nations which never breaks out into overt warfare. Writing in the left-wing weekly *Tribune* in October 1945, Orwell took a pessimistic but somewhat unusual view of the threat posed by nuclear weapons. Instead of the universal destruction feared by writers such as H.G. Wells, Orwell foresaw 'an epoch as horribly stable as the slave empires of antiquity.' The nuclear bomb would make a state 'unconquerable' but at the same time put it into a permanent condition of 'cold war' with its neighbours, the very image of stasis which Orwell was to dramatise in his satirical dystopia *Nineteen Eighty-Four* (1949). In fact, Orwell told his publisher that the idea of the three power blocs in his famous novel came from the 1943 summit meeting in Tehran between Roosevelt, Stalin and Churchill, the first time the three war leaders met together in a conference which helped to shape the world after the war.

In the real world at the end of World War Two, relations between Soviet Russia and the West were chilly but not yet frozen. Only when Stalin realised that the Americans were not going to withdraw troops from Europe did he drop the mask and, by means of threats, coups and manipulation, tighten control over the nations which his armies had liberated from Nazi control. By the late 1940s 'Cold War' had become a generally accepted expression, though sometimes appearing in quotation marks. By the start of the 1950s it had become the status quo, uncomfortable but infinitely preferable to the alternative of 'hot war', and a state of affairs which was to endure for a further 40 years.

Language of Mass Destruction
[American/British: The Nuclear Age]

We can date the beginning of the nuclear age from the first dropping of an atomic bomb on Hiroshima (6 August 1945) or the first detonation of such a weapon at the Los Alamos test site in New Mexico (16 July 1945) or, earlier still, from the setting up of the Manhattan Project, the US code name for the programme to construct an A-bomb (13 August 1942). Or we can go back further to the theoretical work of physicists and chemists in the early years of the 20th century.

But the prospect of atomic weaponry had been foreshadowed by the writer H.G. Wells, even as World War One was breaking out. Like George Orwell, Wells had a remarkable ability not merely to catch the current of the time but also to anticipate it. The era of Queen Victoria had scarcely ended when Wells wrote about the frightening possibilities of aerial warfare (*see* Chapter 1: Things to Come). Then, in *The World Set Free*, a novel published in 1914, Wells talked of: 'The three atomic bombs, the new bombs that would continue to explode indefinitely.' Wells's science may have been sketchy but his prophetic fears were well grounded.

Given the prevalence of the talk about 'weapons of mass destruction' (WMD) in the aftermath of the Iraq War, it is surprising to note the same phrase being used as far back as

1937 in *The Times* in an article foreseeing the 'horror of what another widespread war would mean'. As the Cold War was beginning post-1945 and apprehensions grew about nuclear conflict between east and west, 'atomic bomb' terminology entered the language. Some of it related to the types of weapon: hydrogen, neutron, thermonuclear, plutonium, etc. The most terrifying of these was the sci-fi-style 'doomsday machine', a hypothetical device capable of triggering universal nuclear destruction without human intervention. Such a 'machine' would supposedly act as the ultimate deterrent, since any attacker would inevitably be destroyed together with his target (and everything else).

Other terms connected to the appearance of the bomb or its effects soon became familiar in the aftermath of World War Two. There was the use of the prefix mega- in the grim computation of explosive power (bombs were measured in megatons, one of which is equivalent to a million tons of TNT) and casualties (one megadeath = a million deaths). Before the end of the 1940s the 'mushroom cloud' or the 'fireball' had become shorthand for what was most to be feared for the future. The 'early warning' system might enable you to survive but the poisonous impact of the 'fall-out' would probably condemn you to a lingering death in a horribly changed world.

'Ground zero', the original designation for the place closest to a nuclear blast, was used in reports on the effects of the Hiroshima and Nagasaki bombs. The clinical objectivity of the phrase indicated its military/scientific origin. Although retaining its nuclear associations, 'ground zero' like 'fallout' was also used in a variety of non-nuclear, non-disastrous contexts. Indeed, the phrase became so diluted by general use that it meant not much more than 'square one', as in: 'We're starting at ground zero.' Then came the terrorist attacks of 9/11, the suddenness and traumatic effect of which brought the original sense back into use. There is now a Ground Zero Museum near the World Trade Center site in New York.

Sunlit Uplands

[British: The Beveridge Report/Welfare State]

When Prime Minister Winston Churchill and Clement Attlee, the Deputy Prime Minister and leader of the Labour Party, attended the Potsdam Conference (17 July–2 August 1945) – code-named 'Terminal' and convened near the ruins of Berlin – the two leaders inspected a parade of British soldiers in the conquered city. With some anxiety, a British diplomat observed that of the two men it was the Labour leader who was greeted with the louder cheers. Attlee's reception was one of several straws in the political wind as World War Two drew to a close.

With the war over, at least in the West, Britain no longer needed a coalition government. A general election was impending and only the far-sighted few considered the possibility that Churchill and his Conservative Party might lose. The general view was: how could a grateful nation kick out of office the man who had guided them to victory? Why should a war-weary country risk turning from a supremely charismatic leader to one who was regarded as dry and colourless and, furthermore, a socialist? Even Stalin expected Churchill to win, observing to the British Prime Minister that, to judge by Attlee's expression, 'I do not think he looks forward avidly to taking over your authority.'

On 25 July the British delegation left Potsdam for the election back at home. The other Allied nations, including the

Russians, awaited Churchill's certain return in a couple of days. But when the figures came in, the Labour majority over the Conservatives in parliament amounted to 180 seats; a landslide result. It was Clement Attlee who flew back to Potsdam as Prime Minister while Churchill moved out from Downing Street into Claridge's Hotel.

One name, William Beveridge, and the committee report which bears his name, symbolised the change which gradually overtook Britain during the war years and produced a Labour majority at the end of them. An academic and briefly a Liberal MP, William Beveridge (1879–1963) was an economist who, from early in his career, had been interested in unemployment. His report on Social Insurance and Allied Services was published in 1942. Beveridge went beyond his brief, which was merely to tidy up the mess of existing social insurance schemes (inadequately covering unemployment, sickness, etc.), and proposed instead a universal programme that would protect people from 'cradle to grave', a phrase widely used from the early 1940s.

Beveridge – as the Report was known – became the blueprint for the welfare state (a term first used in print in 1941) that was to shape British history for the next half-century and beyond. While Britain was fighting a war overseas, Beveridge identified a more insidious enemy at home. Almost in the style and language of Victorian preacher, he characterised the 'evils' which stood in the way of social betterment as squalor, disease, ignorance, want and idleness.

When the report was first presented to parliament in March 1943 it was given a grudging welcome with many Conservatives agitating about how it would all be paid for and, behind them, employers complaining about the cost of their contributions. It took time but compromises to the original proposals and the election of the Attlee government in 1945 meant that most of Beveridge's ideas were eventually implemented.

It is significant that the Beveridge report was published soon after the battle of El Alamein, the first British victory following a string of defeats and setbacks. Though it failed to impress the more reactionary politicians, Beveridge's vision caught the imagination of a public that could glimpse the possibility of victory and even dream of a better order of things when the fighting was over. But Beveridge was also a significant instrument of propaganda to be wielded against the other side. For a nation to produce a blueprint for how postwar society might work more justly carried the implicit message that that nation must be expecting to win the war. With pardonable exaggeration, Tom Hopkinson, the left-leaning editor of *Picture Post* magazine, wrote:

> *It [the Beveridge Report] appeared first as a mighty weapon of war, more powerful than thousands of Churchill tanks, having greater destructive force than hundreds of the dive-bombers we do not make.*

The Germans thought the same. When the BBC, back in December, began to make the Beveridge Report and its meaning known to oppressed Europe, the Nazis were beside themselves. What became of their promised New Order if Britain should decide upon a real one? As *Picture Post* succinctly put it (6 March 1943): 'The report – designed to cast out fear from the people of Britain – brought terror to the rulers of Germany, Italy, Japan.'

Resetting the Clock

[German: *Stunde Null*, **'Zero Hour'/**
Vergangenheitsbewältigung,
'coming to terms with the past']

Having emerged victorious from World War Two, we Britons can scarcely imagine the psychological impact that defeat and capitulation had on the population of Germany. Quite aside from all the material privations that the war had brought (a common heritage of the conflict throughout Europe), in addition Germans had to confront the reality of having lived under, and in many cases actively supported, a regime that had perpetrated appalling crimes against humanity.

Stunde Null derives from military strategy, and basically denotes the precise time at which Hitler's forces formally surrendered to the Allies – midnight on 8 May 1945, in a tent on the Lüneburg Heath in Lower Saxony. But beyond this, in the light of the living nightmare that Germany had passed through in the preceding 12 years, for many it took on the significance of a new beginning. A chance, after the obscene aberration of the 'Third Reich', to restore their country to a trajectory guided by the cultural legacy of such humane, rational and civilised figures as Lessing, Kant, Goethe and Heine.

For most, of course, these high-minded ideals were far from uppermost in their thoughts. Day-to-day survival was the priority. The immediate postwar period spawned its own clutch of terms which express the hardship being suffered. Perhaps the most famous of these is *Trümmerfrauen*, the 'rubble women' whose Herculean efforts in clearing away shattered infrastructure quite literally prepared the ground for the country's revival. Less familiar is the verb *fringsen*, a word from Cologne dialect meaning 'to pilfer' (especially food). It was coined from the name of the then-Catholic Archbishop of the Rhineland city, Cardinal Josef Frings (1887–1978), who, in his New Year's sermon of 1946, sanctioned every desperate individual in his flock to: 'take what he needs to preserve his life and health, if he cannot obtain it through other means.'

For postwar German writers and artists, 'zero hour' emphatically did not mean wiping the slate clean, in the sense of starting again as though nothing had happened. To the contrary, it meant wrestling with what had taken place, and laying bare every last painful step leading up to and resulting from Hitler's disastrous accession to power. The sociologist and philosopher Theodor Adorno wrote in 1949 that 'to write poetry after Auschwitz is barbaric', but his famous dictum, far from consigning all artistic endeavour to the dustbin of history, was aimed precisely at any unthinking resumption of German culture with no cognisance or processing of recent history. In particular, the left-leaning circle of writers known as *Gruppe 47* (Group 47) made coming to terms with the (Nazi) past – *Vergangenheitsbewältigung* – an article of faith. Cologne writer Heinrich Böll's early short stories and novels (*And Never Said a Word*, 1953; *The Bread of the Early Years*, 1955) lay bare the complicity of many institutions, including the Catholic Church, in the fascist project, while Günter Grass's *Danzig Trilogy*, most notably *The Tin Drum* (1959), takes a scathing and scabrous look at ordinary Germans' response to the Hitler regime. Both authors went on to win the Nobel Prize for Literature.

Many commentators on postwar Germany have marvelled at

the remarkable feat of the so-called *Wirtschaftswunder* ('economic miracle'), which saw German industry and commerce rise from the ashes by the early 1960s and begin its ascent to European preeminence. Even more remarkable and praiseworthy, though, was this willingness, this urgency, to confront the past and ask difficult questions. It is something that neither Japan nor Italy has ever attempted; we are treated to the regular, and unedifying, spectacle of Japanese politicians paying homage at a shrine to their country's war criminals, while in 2003 Silvio Berlusconi described Mussolini's fascist regime as a 'benign dictatorship'.

A Craving for Culture
[British: CEMA/The Third Programme]

The philosopher C.E.M. Joad (1891–1953) was a regular on the immensely popular wartime BBC radio programme *The Brains Trust*, a panel of experts who answered listeners' questions of all kinds ('What is the basis of a happy marriage?'; 'How does a fly land on a ceiling?') The programme was initially aimed at men and women in the services but soon outgrew its original remit: at its peak over a quarter of the UK population tuned in. It was responsible for hundreds of imitation discussion groups up and down the country as well as the forerunner of postwar panel shows like the still-running *Any Questions?* Yet Professor Joad was generally dismissive of popular culture, writing in *The New Statesman* in 1941: 'What, then, has been the distinctive cultural expression of the English genius during the years 1939 to 1941 ... The answer is "light music".'

For all Joad's disdain, the war years saw a surge of interest

215

in what would then have been called the highbrow arts, especially concerts. This was as much the result of government policy as of people's need for something more meaningful or uplifting in difficult times. The Council for the Encouragement of the Arts (CEMA) was formally set up in 1940, with the aim of lifting morale as well as furthering public education, right down to the most local level. The Council was an energetic promoter of music. According to Robert Hewison in his cultural history of the war years, *Under Siege* (1977): 'CEMA held 4,449 concerts in 1943, in 1944 concerts and recitals were taking place at the rate of seventy a week in factories, and thirty a week in churches and village halls.' In 1945, the (Labour) government decided that CEMA should continue after the end of the war under the title of the Arts Council of Great Britain.

Another significant, if indirect, cultural legacy of World War Two was the establishment of the BBC Third Programme in 1946. The utilitarian title indicated that it was the third national radio station after the Home Service and the Light Programme.* The Third was always intended to be a grazing ground for highbrows. Sir William Haley, the Director-General of the BBC at the time, said: 'Let it enable the intelligent public to hear the best that has been said or thought or composed in all the world [. . .] Let it be something which has never been attempted hitherto in any country.' The station very soon became identified with a certain style of programme, often obscure or difficult, as well as a certain type of person. Despite the respect and affection in which the Third was held, it was also an easy target for satire. In his novel, *The End of the Affair* (1951), set during the end of the war and its immediate aftermath, Graham Greene has fun with a minor character, a literary reviewer for a little magazine who is inclined to make remarks like: 'Don't be late, Sylvia. There's the Bartók programme on the Third at six-thirty.'

*The Home Service turned into Radio 4 in 1967, at the same time as the Light Programme became Radio 2 and the Third Programme Radio 3.

New World Order
[American/British: Bretton Woods/ NATO/European Union]

The shape of much of the world was dictated by World War Two and its aftermath. The victorious Allies set up various international organisations in the attempt to guarantee global stability or, at least, to avert the conditions which might lead to another and even more catastrophic conflict. The names of these organisations or, more usually, their acronyms and initials would become woven into the history of the next half-century and beyond.

Many in government and academia saw cause and effect in the fact that the worst war in history had broken out after the Great Depression, the disastrous economic crisis of the 1930s. Early on, plans were being laid to ensure that the capitalist economies could be brought into alignment with each other once the fighting was over. A series of monetary negotiations between Britain and America, beginning in 1941, culminated in a conference held in the resort village of Bretton Woods in New Hampshire during July 1944, less than a month after the D-Day landings.

This attempt at regulating the international financial system resulted in the creation of the International Monetary Fund

(IMF) and the World Bank. The Mount Washington Hotel in Bretton Woods, the largest building in the state, hosted 730 delegates from 44 countries but the star attraction was undoubtedly John Maynard Keynes (1883–1946), the English economist who, as early as 1931, was famous enough for his theories to have earned the eponymous term 'Keynesian'. It was Keynes's declining health that caused the conference to be held in the cooler climate of the Rocky Mountains and not in the summer humidity of Washington. Despite this care, Keynes had a minor heart attack two weeks into the conference and died not long afterwards. Yet his theories, particularly on the role of the state in managing national economies, remain highly influential and Bretton Woods lives on as a shorthand term for the postwar financial settlement.

When the Iron Curtain and the Cold War became immovable features of the landscape, the military alliance between several western countries became formalised as the North Atlantic Treaty Organisation (NATO), established in 1949 with the US as the first-among-equals leader. By this time Germany was divided, the old Western zones (i.e. those under the control of the United States, UK and France at the end of the war) becoming the Federal Republic, while the East, under the control of Soviet forces, became the German Democratic Republic (*Deutsche Demokratische Republik*). In 1955, the Soviet Union set up the Warsaw Pact (because it was signed in Warsaw), a counterpart to NATO and an alliance between the eastern bloc countries, with the exception of Yugoslavia. The East–West division persisted until the fall of the Berlin Wall in 1989 and the reunification of Germany in the following year. NATO still exists as a military alliance, with action in such places as Libya (during the 2011 campaign to oust Colonel

Gaddafi), but a large part of its *raison d'être* has gone with the break-up of the old Eastern Bloc.

A process which the war certainly hastened, though it did not cause, was the break-up of the British Empire. The Empire's heyday had been in the Victorian era and the imperial sun was well on its way to setting by the early stages of the 20th century. For all that, the contribution of countries such as Australia, New Zealand, Canada and India to the war effort, in terms of men and resources, was immeasurable. Winston Churchill was the arch-imperialist, describing India as 'the brightest jewel in the crown of empire'. Yet the more powerful members of the Alliance, the United States and the USSR, had no interest in helping Britain preserve its overseas dominions. Indeed, President Roosevelt was actively hostile to old-world imperialism, freely using terms like 'medieval' to describe the system and remarking that the people in (French) Indochina were worse off than they had been before the arrival of the Europeans. In Britain's case, the Empire was translated into the Commonwealth, a term in use from the early 20th century but not really coming into its own until after the end of the war. And it was not until February 1958 that *The Times* noted: 'It is proposed to change the name of Empire Day forthwith to Commonwealth Day.'

From the British – or more accurately, English – point of view, the most contentious legacy of World War Two has been the European Union. Beginning as the European Coal and Steel Community (ECSC) in 1951, its original purpose was to create a harmonised common market for coal and steel among member states. But the treaty setting up the ECSC was never a purely commercial one, since disputes over resources and the rivalry between France and Germany, particularly in the Ruhr, had been one of the factors leading to war. Rather, it was to be a first step to a greater European integration with the aim, in the words of one of its founders, of making 'war [in Europe] not only unthinkable but materially impossible'. The original six member states were Belgium, France, West Germany, Italy, the Netherlands and Luxembourg. As usual, Britain stood on the sidelines or alternatively, in the words of Noel Annan in *Changing Enemies* (1995), threw 'into the gutter the leadership of a European Community that was hers for the asking', with the result that later British attempts to join the European Economic Community (EEC), as it became in 1957, were protracted and even humiliating.

If the principal aim of the much-enlarged European Union (EU), as it is now called, has been to make another European war 'unthinkable' then it has succeeded, just as it has succeeded in areas like the harmonising of employment law. But the UK's membership of the EU has caused civil war among the British political parties, principally for the Conservatives. 'Eurosceptic' is first cited in the dictionary in 1985, not coincidentally at the high point of Mrs Thatcher's hold on Downing Street.

'Don't Mention the War!'
[British: Germanophobia]

The effects of World War Two are still with us. And, arguably, the legacy of the war is stronger – or more carefully preserved – in Britain than in any of the other major countries involved in the conflict, with the possible exception of Russia. Nearly three-quarters of a century after the celebration of VE Day, the publication of books on everything,from the leading figures in the Third Reich to the most arcane corners of Nazism shows no sign of slackening. On the home front, Winston Churchill's life and premiership are the subject of continuous assessment. Every facet of the war is explored. For example, the delayed revelations about Enigma and the Bletchley code-breakers, first emerging in the 1970s, are responsible for dozens of studies and documentaries, and the hold on the national imagination of these stories of British amateurism, eccentricity and high ingenuity is as strong as ever.

We can trace the footprints of the war and its consequences in the most successful series of spy novels ever written. Between 1939 and 1945 Ian Fleming worked in Naval Intelligence, where he exercised his imagination in dreaming up schemes and subterfuges to outwit the enemy. But Fleming's considerable creativity was put to better use when he conjured up the world of James Bond, starting with *Casino Royale* in 1953. Apart from a notorious torture scene, the first Bond novel is quite low-key by comparison with the later extravaganzas. But from the beginning of the series a lot of attention was paid to food and in a style that was intended to make Fleming's British readers salivate. Ordering dinner in the *Hotel Splendide* in company with the heroine/double agent Vesper Lynd, James Bond tells the maître d': 'While mademoiselle is enjoying the strawberries, I will have half an avocado with a little French dressing.' Apart from being a reminder that avocado can come after the main course, the detail evokes a period of continuing rationing in Britain, an era of shortages in which the avocado had an almost exotic appeal. If refined food was a treat, travel was a privilege, even many years after the war had finished. In *Goldfinger* (1959) several pages are devoted to Bond's pursuit of the villain across France, with stops for menus and knowledgeable asides. ('When in doubt, Bond always chose the station hotels.') In the 1950s, such leisurely tourism was rare; any experience of Europe for people less privileged than Ian Fleming would most likely have been confined to their memories of war service abroad.

More specific wartime allusions appear in *Moonraker* (1955) when Sir Hugo Drax, abandoning his pose as an English gentleman, reveals himself to be Graf Hugo von der Drache, a one-time member of the 'Hitlerjugend Werewolves' and now bent on the destruction of London with the nuclear-tipped Moonraker rocket, a much more destructive variant of the V-2. Nearly 10 years later Fleming was still invoking the Nazi stereotype. In *On Her Majesty's Secret Service* (1963) and *You Only Live Twice* (1964), Ernst Stavro Blofeld's sidekick, Irma Bunt, comes straight out of central casting with her 'square wardress face' and her tendency to make remarks like: 'But of course, lieber Ernst. What you decide is always correct.'

In the 50 years since Ian Fleming's death, the potency of the Nazis and their paraphernalia seems undiminished, whether it emerges in the form of tabloid gibes at the Germans or in the more intelligent books and television programmes already mentioned. Commenting on a famous *Daily Mirror* front page which featured footballer Paul Gascoigne in a superimposed World War Two helmet and the headline 'ACHTUNG! SURRENDER! For you Fritz, ze Euro 96 Championship is over', the *New York Times* said:

It could probably be said that the two unifying victories for England in Queen Elizabeth's lifetime have been the war and the 1966 World Cup final at Wembley, in which

the Germans were beaten – accounting for the last major
victory for the creator of the world's favorite sport.
(New York Times, 26/6/96)

On a more serious level, British attitudes towards Germany are still coloured by 1939–45 and the events leading up to those years. Although there is admiration for qualities like efficiency and industriousness, and for the economic miracle (or *Wirtschaftswunder*) by which Germany transformed itself, there is also ambivalence and sometimes unease about an old enemy which is now the most powerful state in Europe.

Bibliography

Non-fiction & memoirs

Noel Annan   *Changing Enemies* (1995)

Mike Brown   *Wartime Britain* (2011)

Michael Burleigh   *Moral Combat: A History of World War II* (2011)

Alan Clark   *Barbarossa* (1965)

Richard Collier   *1940: The World in Flames* (1979)

Paul Devrient *Mein Schüler Hitler* (1975)

Jonathan Fenby   *Alliance* (2006)

Peter Fleming   *Invasion 1940* (1957)

Paul Fussell   *The Great War and Modern Memory* (1975)

   Wartime (1989)

   Doing Battle (1996)

   The Boys' Crusade (2004)

Daniel Goldhagen *Hitler's Willing Executioners: Ordinary Germans and the Holocaust* (1996)

Richard Griffiths   *Fellow Travellers of the Right* (1980)

Max Hastings   *Finest Years* (2009)

Joseph Heller   *Now And Then* (1998)

Robert Hewison   *Under Siege* (1977)

Tom Hopkinson   *Picture Post 1938--50* (1970)

Lucy Hughes-Hallett   The Pike: G*abriele D'Annunzio* (2013)

Mark Jacobson: *The Lampshade: A Holocaust Detective Story from Buchenwald to New Orleans* (2010)

R.V. Jones   *Most Secret War* (1978)

Sidney Kirkpatrick   *Hitler's Holy Relics* (2011)

Victor Klemperer   *LTI – Lingua Tertii Imperii; Notizbuch eines Philologen* (1947)

David Kynaston *Austerity Britain 1945–51* (2007)

David Lampe   *The Last Ditch: Britain's Resistance Plans Against the Nazis* (2007)

Ben MacIntyre   *Double Cross* (2012)

Robert Mackay   *Half the Battle* (2002)

Leonard Mosley   *On Borrowed Time* (1969)

George Orwell   *Why I Write* (1946)

Nicholas Rankin   *Churchill's Wizards* (2008)

Cornelia Schmitz-Berning   *Vokabular des Nationalsozialismus* (1997)

W.G. Sebald   *Luftkrieg und Literatur* (2001)

Studs Terkel   *The Good War: An Oral History of World War Two* (1984)

E.S. Turner   *The Phoney War* (1961)

David Welch   *Propaganda: Power and Persuasion* (2013)

A.E. Wren   *Oddentification: 64 Drawings and Rhymes reprinted from 'The Aeroplane'* (1942)

Fiction

Nigel Balchin   *Darkness Falls from the Air* (1942)
   The Small Back Room (1943)
   Mine Own Executioner (1945)

Heinrich Böll   *Und sagte kein einziges Wort* (1953)
   Das Brot der frühen Jahre (1955)
   Irisches Tagebuch (1957)

Elizabeth Bowen   *The Heat of the Day* (1949)

Agatha Christie   *N or M?* (1941)
Len Deighton   *SS-GB*   (1978)
Ian Fleming   *Casino Royale* (1953)
    Moonraker (1955)
Günter Grass   *Die Blechtrommel* (1959)
    Im Krebsgang (2002)
Graham Greene   *The Ministry of Fear* (1943)
    The End of the Affair (1951)
Robert Harris   *Fatherland* (1992)
Joseph Heller   *Catch 22* (1961)
Hammond Innes   *Wreckers Must Breathe* (1940)
Philip Kerr   *Berlin Noir* (1993)
    If the Dead Rise Not (2009)
George Orwell   *Nineteen Eighty-Four* (1949)
David Piper   *Trial by Battle* (1959)
Philip Roth   *The Plot Against America* (2004)
C.J. Sansom   *Dominion* (2012)
Evelyn Waugh   *Put Out More Flags* (1942)
    Brideshead Revisited (1945)

Reference

Oxford English Dictionary
Oxford Companion to World War II (2001)
Jonathon Greene *Cassell Dictionary of Slang* (1998)
J.L. Hunt & A.G. Pringle   *Service Slang* (1943)
Gordon L. Rottman   *FUBAR: Soldier Slang of World War II* (2007)

Online

for Winston Churchill's speeches: www.winstonchurchill.org

for Franklin Roosevelt's speeches: millercenter.org/president/
speeches

for UK pillbox sites: www.pillbox-study-group.org.uk

Index